UNDEFINED

Shattering the False Reflections of Life

Chaye Benjamin

Acknowledgements

Thank you, God, for this assignment.

Thank you for this gift.

Thank you for this purpose that you burned into my heart so deeply

that I couldn't quit, even when I thought I should.

Thank you for the strength to stand against the fear of rejection.

Thank you for allowing me to be a vessel for you.

Thank you for taking the pain in this and turning it into freedom.

To my husband, my Music

If I were to write a book about how much

I love you and how grateful I am to have someone like

you standing by my side and cheering me on,

it would outweigh this book in words by the thousands.

Thank you for riding through this life with me,

for being strong enough to tame me,

for praying for me, for trusting me,

for showing me that I can trust you,

and for deciding to still be my friend.

To Coach Sarah,

Thank you for pushing me and fighting against doubt with me.

Thank you for those three weeks.

Thank you for all that you've done to make this happen.

And thank you for making me say to myself every day,

"Iamawriter."

TABLE OF CONTENTS

INTRODUCTION

"There are different chapters in everyone's lives that they could use to fill a book. But when you sit back and think … aren't you grateful for some of the chapters that won't be in yours? And even if you have been through hell and back, aren't you grateful that you're still alive to even write the book?!"

- My Facebook status from November 17, 2009

There is a song that says, "As I look back over my life, and I think things over, I can truly say…" Stop. What would you say? If you took a look back over some of the most notable moments of your life, how would you sum things up? After you look back, would you say that your identity was formed from those moments, or have you become someone beyond who life (and the people in it) says you should be?

Finding the freedom to be authentically you takes courage. To be able to be who you really want to be and believe yourself to be takes a strength that is both organic and developed. It takes making the decision to not just survive, but to thrive in the middle of or once the break of day is seen through the harsh winds and rains of the storms of life. Oftentimes, it is the person with that kind of strength and spirit that will use life to find who they are by looking back at how they managed each obstacle and hurdle they have had to jump over. They may not have it all figured out, but life wasn't able to knock them down, and they identified their strength in the midst of turmoil. On the contrary, for the person who has a hard time finding strength as life continues to throw its hardest blows and win each round, they will find themselves asking life who they are supposed to be. They have become constrained by life, unable to be anything other than who or what life has permitted them to be.

I was that person. I became exactly what life told me to be, based on every negative moment and the projected thoughts and feelings of other people toward me. Not knowing how to manage my emotions, build strength from my struggles, or push past barriers and setbacks, I often deemed myself unfit, unworthy, and even unnecessary at times. However, as I write these words, I speak from a place of strength and survival. The things I have endured (both big and small) almost won the fight for my life on several occasions, all because of my state of mind. See, it doesn't matter what you go through; what matters is how you go through it.

You are about to go on a journey through the different chapters of my life and walk through the detailed pages that outline each moment which left lasting effects on my mind, body, soul, and spirit. As you read, you will see there were times I thought I would never make it out, times I thought I could never be free. I tried to define who I was, based on each situation, the reactions of those involved, and who I believed I was supposed to be. Although it took many years, much heartache, and even more prayer, I finally made it to the place where I could identify myself as Free. Free from the pressures I felt as an adolescent and as an adult to fit in. Free from the thoughts that tormented my mind night after night, telling me that I would never make it out or amount to much more than the mistakes I'd made and the issues I'd created. Free from the lie that the only way I would be loved was if I were someone else. Only God could untie the knots that held me bound to so many lies and misconceptions and show me my true identity, but he couldn't do that until I stopped trying to figure things out on my own and ignored the voices of everyone else.

Finding your true identity will never be possible until you become free from your past, the opinions and expectations of others, and what life tells you that you should be. Come take a walk with me; you may find yourself within the pages of my story. Find out what it took for me to find my freedom and the barriers I had to knock down before I could claim it. If you are searching for your true identity, let me tell you how I found mine and learned to not just accept it, but love it. If you know who you are, I invite you to take a look into the life of someone who wasn't able to find themselves as easily and almost allowed even the smallest things to take them out. Life happens to everyone, but everyone handles it differently, and not everyone knows how to be or who to be when life stands against them.

Ask me how I know.

CHAPTER 1
Priceless

I think I wanna write for a minute.

Can I write for a minute,

Capture all my thoughts and secrets in a book?

A notebook or maybe a diary, thoughts just for me

Cuz if anybody knew the secrets

That lie within the pages of me,

What would they think?

Criticized immediately, turned away indefinitely

All because they read the book,

And now they know the real me

Or who I used to be

But would they see that,

Or would their visions be distorted

Since my thoughts have been sorted

Taken from a place in my mind and put between the lines

Of the pages of my life?

They called me "Bird." This name was given to me because of how happy, free, and full of life I was. Obviously, it was a name that didn't fit me because none of these things truly defined me at the time. Though I exhibited them, they were all masks. From a distance I had watched friends, family, and acquaintances that seemed to have life figured out and had pulled themselves together over the years, but not me. I always felt stuck, and I didn't know whether I should put the gear in drive or reverse or turn left or right, in order to finally jolt out of the thick mess I'd driven myself into. I knew there had to be a way out of this, but how? And who was going to help me pull or push? Truth be told, it took some work ... some hard work and constant affirming that I actually was worth more than what I thought of myself and that my identity was made up of more than just the masks I used to cover up my mistakes. Beyond the masks I had created for myself, I was given different identities based on what people [thought they] knew about me. They based my identity on what they saw me do or how they saw me act, though I was never really just one of those things. For the person who believes they are limited in talent or ability, it may seem great to have so many sides to yourself that you don't even know which one to be identified as, but not for me. I often felt like a prisoner of my own interests and abilities. Yes, Bird was what they called me, but that wasn't how I defined myself.

As a teenager, I thought nothing too deep of life, except that I wanted to enjoy it, and I wanted the people I was surrounded by to enjoy me. So every day, I made it my mission to make sure that, in every situation and with every person I became connected to, they never left my presence unsatisfied. At thirteen years old, though I was still young, naïve, and inexperienced in many things, there was one area I was learning to master — the art of seduction. As the youngest, I had watched my sisters and my older cousins go through the "normal" stages of growing up and maturing. It was then that I quickly caught on to this masterful concept that I too was a young woman with a unique ability. I had realized that, though my looks were only average, I could develop what I had heard them call "sex appeal," and it would make me attractive to both guys and girls (though I never had a desire to take a relationship any further than just friends with a female). However, with insecurity guiding my lost, adolescent mind, I found myself making the worst decision of my life, a decision only maturity would be able to reveal to me as the worst one.

I had a deep desire to be accepted by Church, the one boy in whom my emotions had been invested for many years. I had allowed him (not once, but twice) to touch a place in me that should have remained reserved for the one I truly loved and became legally and spiritually bonded with much later in life. Church was the guy that captivated my attention for as long as I could remember, and because we grew up together, everyone always told us that marriage between the two of us was inevitable. It all seemed pretty harmless — puppy love, at its best — until everything took a serious turn. That turn happened the day Church came over to hang out (which was not uncommon), and after a couple hours of nonchalant conversation, he eventually slipped in the idea of allowing him to be my "first." Never had I been so nervous around him. I had never allowed him (or any other boy) to get that far with me. What if he didn't like what he saw once my clothes were off? Could I hide under the blankets? What if he thought I was no good?

Would he tell his friends? Most importantly, would my mom find out? What if God told her and my grandmother that I had defiled myself by giving my body to someone before marriage and at this age? There was an innocent (and maybe naïve) image that I carried, and although it was hard to keep up at times, I didn't want that to be tarnished in the eyes of my family.

Church had brought up the idea about sex before, but I had always rejected his advances and laughed them off as a joke, and we had never been in a position where the opportunity was actually possible, until now.

Regardless of how I felt, with my mind racing in a million different directions, fear gripped me like never before. I was so afraid that he would think I was scared or immature for rejecting him yet again. A few of my friends had told me their vivid stories about their first sexual experiences, so in addition to wanting to impress him, I wanted to see what all the hype was about, so I gave in to temptation.

(Well, let's just say, I didn't find out the first time … or the second.)

There was no word I could find to describe how it felt to force myself to lie there half-dressed and uncomfortable, un-aroused and scared. So scared and uncomfortable, that, by the time I talked myself into relaxing and trying to enjoy what was happening, it was over.

Was that it?

The moment I had anticipated, which was supposed to be beautiful, was over, just like that, and I was left lying across the bed, wishing the pain would go away.

Was *that* it?

I thought, for sure, I had ruined the entire experience for myself because he seemed to be satisfied. So, what about me? Why wasn't I satisfied? I convinced myself that, if I had handled the situation better by being a bit easier and more mature, then the feelings of being unsatisfied and un-romanced would have been nonexistent. Still, somewhere deep in my mind, I felt that my feelings were absent because maybe, at thirteen years old, I just wasn't ready to take this step. I would come to find that my mind knew best when I allowed him to convince me a second time and once again ... nothing.

The absence of pleasure was not all that left me unsatisfied. I expected there would be pain; after all, it was my first time having sex, and I had heard enough to know that it would be a bit uncomfortable. My disappointment came about with the absence of emotion from Church. He didn't take the time out to make me comfortable (other than telling me to relax). He didn't make me feel beautiful and wanted, and he didn't even touch or kiss me or any other part of my body (which no one had to tell me was supposed to be part of the ordeal). What hurt even more than the pain of sex itself was, after everything happened (for the second time), Church seemed to fall off the face of the earth, my earth. He didn't give an explanation for the distance he had created between us, and it left me feeling swindled and betrayed. Questions circled around my mind: Did he ask me to have sex with him simply to prove that he could get me to say yes? Was I unknowingly the center of some heinous bet made between him and his friends that he could take my virginity?

Embarrassment wreaked havoc through my body, to the point where I couldn't even look at him, let alone speak to him whenever I saw him from then on. He seemed to be unbothered by the entire situation because he had no problem saying hello or talking to me, even when he saw it made me uncomfortable. It was apparent that, from that moment, the dynamics of our relationship had completely changed, along with my outlook on life, myself, and the strength of my spirit.

Over the years, as we grew up and matured, it was revealed that, aside from being just as young as I was, Church was dealing with emotional distress and some pretty heavy life experiences himself. He was trying to find his way in life, just as I was, so I really couldn't blame him for his inability to pacify the unspoken desires in a young girl to be genuinely wanted. However, it was that moment in time and the feelings I was left to deal with that forced me to believe I needed to take on a confident, dominant identity, so I would never be left unsatisfied or emotionally devastated ever again.

I decided it was time to put into practice the things I had learned by watching my older sisters and cousins. Therefore, wherever I went, I made it my business to walk with a sexy confidence. Once I noticed the curiosity in the damsel behind this captivating walk and the mysterious smile growing, I discovered the power I held and used it on each guy that expressed interest in me or flashed a simple smile my way. The more I walked, the more I learned how to pull them in, and for those that I was able to hook, I used them to boost my self-confidence all the more. As seductive and desirable as I made myself seem, looking and acting this "easy" warranted various encounters that did nothing more than leave me with an even lower sense of self-worth.

My expectation was that the power I walked and talked with would make me appear to have a dominant personality, never allowing me to be played again. The truth was, what appeared to be power was really just a self-made, lifelike mask I wore to cover my insecurities. I remained hidden behind this truth and determined that I would make my dominance appear real to everyone, including myself. It seemingly worked until, one day, during my first year of high school, my lack of true dominance and strength led me into the clutches of what almost became a traumatic experience.

While waiting for my friends to finish with their after-school programs and clubs, I wandered outside to find a group of guys, who had once attended the school, hanging around. I knew most of them, but then I was personally introduced to Pressure when he noticed my walk and my piercing stare, once eye contact was made. I thought, *This is my chance to shine and prove myself.* After luring him in with my conversation, it wasn't long until he was leaving his group behind to take a walk with me. We casually walked back into the school, up the ramped hallway, and through the open doors of the dark, vacant auditorium, which was situated in a secluded corner of the school. Thinking I was simply going to tease him, test him, and be done with him, I quickly found that he had other plans. After I felt as if I had made my point about what I was capable of, I began to walk away, but he snatched me back against the wall and began to kiss and bite all over my neck while grabbing at my breasts. It seemed as if there was more than one person attacking me, as his hands were going all over my body, and I wasn't fast enough to block them. I was much smaller than he was, so the more I fought, the more force he used, leaving me feeling powerless. The fight seemed to last forever, and I was growing more and more scared by the minute until I finally screamed, "STOP!" so loudly, my voice echoed throughout the huge room, bouncing off the rows of chairs and hitting the blackened stage.

Afraid of getting caught, Pressure quickly let go of me and exited the room, but not before calling me everything except my name, laughing, and telling me what he thought of me in so many words. The most impactful words left ringing in my ears were: *"You ain't even worth it."* Now left alone in the dark corner, I collapsed onto the hard, cold floor, with tears waiting for their permission to begin streaming down my face. Though the entire ordeal left me feeling a bit scared, there was no way that I was going to let anyone see me break. I sat for a bit longer, but once I gathered the courage, I ran to find my friends. Once we all came together, I never spoke a word about it, on that day or any of the days that followed.

From then on, I felt like a failure. There were also other moments when I felt my walk didn't mesmerize the way I had hoped or how I thought it had in the beginning, so I became stuck in my negative mind. I wondered what was wrong with me and why the interest guys showed in me always seemed to fade after a while. It was as if, no matter how hard I tried or how much I practiced to perfect my skill, I just didn't feel as if I could make myself attractive enough to be wanted. This harsh conclusion sent me into a downward spiral of low self-esteem, believing that it was obviously my physical appearance that caused them to become uninterested. Not to mention, I was at the age where fitting in with the crowd was important, so when I wasn't accepted among certain groups of girls either, it began to distort my view of myself all the more.

Author's Love Note: *It's so easy to count the opinions and actions of others as facts when your outlook of your own self is diminished and you're not sure of who you really are. No matter what race, age, or gender you are, never allow the unprincipled opinions of someone else to ruin your opinion of yourself. Trying to measure up to the world's standard of who you should be is next to impossible. Build yourself, love yourself, challenge yourself, and walk in the confidence you deserve to have, according to your morals and beliefs. You and I may not share the* *same beliefs or have the same religion; I am a God-chaser (Christian), and as such, I try to walk out my life every day, according to the Word of God (the Bible). Even if this isn't your belief, let me share a passage with you always has helped me feel better about myself:*

PSALMS 139:13-18 (New International Version)

13 For you created my inmost being;

you knit me together in my mother's womb.

14 I praise you because I am fearfully and wonderfully made;

your works are wonderful,

I know that full well.

15 My frame was not hidden from you

when I was made in the secret place,

when I was woven together in the depths of the earth.

16 Your eyes saw my unformed body;

all the days ordained for me were written in your book before one of them came to be.

17 How precious to me are your thoughts, God!

How vast is the sum of them!

18 Were I to count them,

they would outnumber the grains of sand—

when I awake, I am still with you.

No matter what you believe, or your religion, your history, your thoughts and ideas, God's hands have wonderfully constructed you, and you are breathing the breath of life that He has breathed into you. All He wants is for you to see you the way that He does — as a masterpiece. Once you begin to look at yourself this way, nothing that anyone else says will even matter, and you will begin to handle yourself as the masterful piece of art that you are.

I was a priceless jewel, which deserved to be handled in the most delicate fashion. However, at this age, with no father present to pour into a young, budding teenage girl (to remind me of how beautiful and precious

I was), I had a hard time seeing myself the way that I should have and found myself giving away the most precious gift I carried. No, an absent father did not cause me to go the way that I ultimately chose to go, but it definitely made it much harder for me to understand how a young woman should expect a young man to treat her and how I should view myself. Everyone handles the absence of a parent differently, and I happened to be one of the ones who didn't handle it so well. Desperately wanting to be noticed and desired, I decided to keep working on myself. I vowed to never have another encounter like the one at school, one that left me feeling weak, vulnerable, insignificant, and unwanted. My mind didn't even remain stuck on the fact that I was almost completely taken advantage of, but the fact that I was deemed "not worth the time." What I didn't realize was that the thing I was subconsciously searching for — the acceptance I needed — would not come from some young boy who thought the world of my body.

There was a need that I was looking to fulfill, but I didn't know where it was going to come from, so I continued my search for acceptance. Not long before my sixteenth birthday, as my mind and imagination began to expand, I, once again, found myself in one compromising position after another, with some being about as serious as the encounter with Pressure at school. I tried to make and stick to the decision to never allow myself to get caught up or fall for anyone else, but because of my emotional desperation and pain, it didn't work. I touched them and they touched me. I fell hard and they fell off. However, even with all of the emotions brought about with each encounter, after my first sexual experience with Church, I remained turned off by the idea of "going all the way" with anyone else. This was the cause of most of the negative reactions I received from the guys I came in contact with, but I had made up in my mind to never allow another boy to stick his hand (or anything else) in my cookie jar.

That is ... until I finally met him.

CHAPTER 2
The Bandaged Heart

It was 1996, my first year of middle school, when a chance meeting turned into a full-on, heart-pounding crush. His name was Music. I often saw him among a group of guys and girls who all lived in the same neighborhood or close by, but he knew nothing of me, except that I was the little sister of one of the older girls they all crushed on. Middle school seemed like an alternate universe, and I didn't know who I was supposed to be or become, so I masked my insecurity with silliness. This was not the best way to be noticed by the guy I noticed all the time. As uncool as it was for my big sister, my mom insisted that my big sister take me everywhere she went. Secretly, I loved going everywhere with her because, not only was there more of a chance I would get to see Music, but being her little sister and hanging out with the older kids was what rewarded me respect and protection by the time I reached high school. Music and I were not officially introduced until the year 2000, during my sophomore year and his junior year in high school. He had grown up so much in just four years. He was now one of the captains of our high school football team, cute, and listed among the boys most girls wanted. As for me, I had grown up a bit, stepped into the teenage world (a bit late), had begun to come out of my shell, and had created an identity for myself, instead of just being known as "little sister."

As it turned out, Music and I had mutual friends that would all hang out together, until eventually, we all became one big group. We ended up seeing each other all the time — him in his dirty uniform after a football game, and me, in my short, pleated skirt and hair bows after a basketball game. Typical high school love story, right? Well, I'll spare you the fairytale scene because things didn't exactly play out the way Walt Disney's imagination would have conceptualized it. I thought it was such a privilege to be accepted by him and our friends; I finally felt noticed, and they never required me to be anything more than just myself. However, with insecurity and early emotional experiences taking me up and down a winding staircase of masked identities, this made finding my true identity difficult, so I never stepped into the person I really was. I loved to do so many things, and I was actually good at them, but what I could never figure out was which "me" I was supposed to be or which thing I was supposed to choose. So the real question was ... who was I?

Growing up in a strict Christian home meant I didn't experience the same freedom as my friends. They would always return to school and talk about which party they had attended, who was there, and how long it had lasted, while I stood by wishing to have only been a fly on the wall. Trying to fit in seemed next to impossible when I couldn't even offer my own opinion about a house party or any other seemingly normal high school shenanigans. I felt out of place.

When I wasn't allowed to go certain places and got questioned by my friends about it, I felt as if they would no longer want to be bothered with me. When they stopped asking me to go here and there, I felt as if I had been dishonorably discharged from the group.

When they decided to change plans to accommodate me, I felt like a burden.

When something would go wrong while we were out, I felt it was my fault. Though none of this had ever been expressed to me, I wholeheartedly believed that these feelings were being expressed behind my back.

The fear and feelings of becoming an outcast prompted another personality change, and I began to act as if nothing ever bothered me. The truth, however, was that I was beginning to break on the inside. Hiding my true emotions, with no true identity, gave birth to anger. There were times I turned from Jekyll to Hyde with the snap of a finger. Why did I feel such a void that brought about bitterness, making me feel so deeply hurt and angry? Though I was never really able to link my anger to a cause, one area of hurt I knew I was still bound by, for years, was the guilt and pain of losing my father ... twice.

As a little girl, I would always love on my father; I always wanted to be in his lap. I hold sweet memories of him loving and kissing on me and all of us being a happy family in our beautiful three-level townhome, with all our friends living in the same neighborhood. From the point of view of a little girl, life was great, so when my sisters and I moved out of the house with just my mother, leaving my father behind, my perfect world crumbled. Loss #1.

Being the youngest in the house, at eight years old, no one explained to me why we had to leave Daddy behind, though I don't think I would have understood anyway. As the years went on, the unconditional love that little girl had for her father diminished and was replaced with an anger I couldn't understand and the harsh opinions of others concerning him. Overhearing phone conversations and quiet talks between my mother and my oldest sister caused curiosity to set in. I needed answers but was too afraid to ask for them. So with a lack of details and information, I drew my own conclusion that whatever took place was his fault. There were times when we were forced to see him, and I would hate it and wondered why we even had to go. He didn't deserve to see us. While visiting, he would make promises to us that were never fulfilled, and he would say that he loved us, but because I didn't believe it, I never reciprocated it. He often said he would visit, but his plans would change. He would call and try to talk to me, but I wasn't eager to answer or return his phone calls. My sister finally helped me to understand that our father was sick. What I began to see before my eyes was the evidence that his sickness was very serious, as many of his bodily functions had begun to stop working, one by one. What I felt in my heart, however, was that he deserved it. I now understood what it felt like to secretly hate the very person that brought you into this world.

Then came the darkest day of October 2001. While the world was still mourning the tragedies of September 11th, my entire world was shattered, but not because of the acts of terrorism. The battle my father had been in with his health for so many years had finally taken his body to a point of no return, and he was placed in hospice care. At that time, I didn't realize what hospice care was; I assumed it was just a fancy hospital or home for those who needed 24-hour care. I didn't even know how he got there or whose decision it was to put him there, but when I found out what hospice care actually was, my heart sank into my stomach. The memory of that day and that time will always remain in my mind.

While sitting in my room in the middle of the afternoon one day, the ring of our home phone echoed through the walls; it was a phone call from the hospice care facility where he was staying. My oldest sister went to speak with my other sister, who then came and spoke to me and tried to gently bring me to the harsh reality that this really was the end. My heart sank just a bit deeper; I didn't know what to say or do. Our mother was out of town, so I made the decision not to go and see him until she got back, even with my sisters warning me that I may not have that long.

When my mother returned, she made her way to see him, as did my sisters once again, but I never built up the courage to go. Finally, after talking to my sister about how serious this was and my mom basically telling me that I had no choice, I made a trip with her to the hospice care facility. I was still holding on to the idea — and maybe the hope — that this would be like any other visit to a regular hospital.

As we walked through the double doors to the hallway where his room was, the air was stale and empty, and an eerie feeling came over me. The hallway was long, secluded, and dim, with one of the fluorescent lights flickering in the ceiling. Usually, there were stretchers and nurses' carts, materials, posters, and a bit more life and happiness in a hospital, but then I remembered ... this wasn't that kind of place. People didn't come here with the hopes of eventually getting better; they came here for a painless, peaceful exit. I kept my eyes focused on the flickering light, as my mother's shoes clicked across the floor, echoing in the silence. From the ride in the car to our check-in to our walk down the hall, I maintained my disposition and nonchalant attitude. I was the "strong one," so there was no way I was going to break over this. However, once we arrived at his room, that all changed. Suddenly terrified, I stepped inside his room and looked at the man I had known as my father for the past fifteen years. He was now taking his last breaths. Shaking and nervous, I touched his hand, which was now cold and thin, and examined the rest of his frail body. My sisters had told me they had been able to speak to him, and he had responded quietly; he had even spoke to my mother, but by the time I finally got there, he was unresponsive. With tears now filling my eyes, I touched his hand again and whispered, "Daddy, I love you, too," and backed out of the room and into the hall to gather myself and wait for my mother to finish speaking with the resident nurse.

Quickly wiping my face and squeezing out a smile, I graciously thanked the nurse after she escorted my mother into the hall, and we finally left. On the way home, my mother talked to me about what was going to happen and asked if I was okay. I reassured her that I would be fine, but the truth was, each of the pieces of my already broken heart were shattering. When we got home, I still acted as if everything was fine when my sisters asked how I was feeling. After speaking with them just a few minutes, I went up to my room and sat on my bed in silence. Not more than an hour had gone by before our mother received the phone call we all had been dreading. My father had died. He had died, and I had never told him I was sorry. I don't know if he had heard me say "I love you." I didn't get to look into his eyes one last time and smile at him. His last memories of me were of anger, hate, and disgust, and now ... he was gone forever. Loss #2.

How could I do such a thing and be such a person that would send someone to his grave with such an unfond memory of me? I can't put into words the pain of losing my father, but I felt as if I was now the one who didn't deserve to be sad. I couldn't even look past what I believed about him or the fact that he really did still love me or that he was still a human being who deserved love, even through his mistakes. It is said that forgiveness is for you, not the other person, because it allows your soul to be free, but for the other person, it also gives them another chance at your love. My one wish became that I would have had the chance for both me and my father to experience this liberation. Instead, I lived with guilt, regret, and pain for so long that it produced fits of rebellion and rage; I would lash out and spit words of fire at anyone who challenged me. My new identity was not one that many embraced, but I no longer cared what anyone thought about me because I didn't think much of myself.

Blue

Words ring out — a voice box, not from the mouth

But from the soul and of the spirit

Pain so loud, the deaf can hear it.

I fear it,

That all too familiar place of no peace and uncertainty,

Feeling like you're alone ...

But everybody knows your name

Living like a celebrity without the fame

Wishing that someone would see my tears

Dry them; someone calm my fears

Hoping that someone would help, but it seems

They devour my plans and steal my dreams

Wanting to lean, wanna trust and depend

On someone ... but not one friend

Can give me peace or understand me

The way I need ... no one can handle me ...

Author's Love Note: *People express hurt, pain, bitterness, anger, low self-confidence, and many other negative emotions in many different ways. Some try to mask it, some express it by acting out, some express it by displaying an attitude of being conceited, and some simply seek attention ... any type of attention.*

For those of you reading this book who have overcome any, many, or even all of these emotionally-charged, outward expressions of inward pain, I applaud you, but don't forget how it once felt to be there. Oftentimes, people "get free" and forget what it was like to be in that place, and this causes them to look down on those who may still be struggling in that very area. God allowed you to go through the things you did, so you could help someone else get through to life on the other side. Look beyond their ugly disposition and see the cry for help (or even for a simple hug), screaming from the inside.

Likewise, for those of you that may still be dealing with deeply-rooted, emotional injuries, this does not have to be what defines you. The hurt, pain, anger, bitterness, unforgiveness, and sadness is not who you are, and you don't have to claim it. There may even be some of you who don't realize that you have taken on these negative traits, but you may have heard it once or twice from someone else, which caused you to question their accusations. It can be hard to recognize what vibe you give off, especially if you have made a practice of covering it up or suppressing your feelings. This is why there are so many scriptures and passages in the Bible that constantly remind us to "examine ourselves." The key to walking in victory is working with God and praying for and with one another.

James 5:9, 16 (New Living Translation)

9 Don't grumble about each other, brothers and sisters, or you will be judged. For look—the Judge is standing at the door!

16 Confess your sins to each other and pray for each other so that you may be healed. The earnest prayer of a righteous person has great power and produces wonderful results.

1 Timothy 2:1 (New Living Translation)

1 I urge you, first of all, to pray for all people. Ask God to help them; intercede on their behalf, and give thanks for them.

Matthew 11:28-30 (New Living Translation)

28 Then Jesus said, "Come to me, all of you who are weary and carry heavy burdens, and I will give you rest.

29 Take my yoke upon you. Let me teach you, because I am humble and gentle at heart, and you will find rest for your souls.

30 For my yoke is easy to bear, and the burden I give you is light."

I grew up in the church, but I knew nothing about handing anything over to God; in order to deal with the pain I felt on the inside, I inflicted pain ... on myself. The deeper the pain, the more my anger grew, and soon enough, I was coming home with bruised and bloody knuckles from punching walls, mirrors, lockers, and just about any inanimate object that I could physically take my aggression out on. Though I maintained my silly and loud character with my friends, when my anger boiled up, I threatened people in school and out. I made it publicly known that I feared no one and dared anyone to try me. This became my new identity, how I defined myself. However, the truth of the matter was, I was actually afraid to get into a fight. It was true that there really was no one that I was afraid of, but with the damage I had done to both my knuckles and a few things they came in contact with, I was afraid that I would lose control and really hurt someone. I knew the feeling of deep, emotional pain — so deep, it felt physical — and I knew I never wanted to inflict that kind of pain on anyone else, so I took it on instead.

It wasn't long before going home with bruised hands became tiresome, so learning to channel it differently became my next mission. Though my attitude remained, I decided that I was tired of hurting myself to spare everyone else, so I brought back to life the flirtatious, sexy girl I once learned to be. I was a few years older and had a bit more experience under my belt, and my body was finally looking how I had always wished. I just knew, this time around, I would be deemed "worth it." I made the switch from wild, loud, and angry to wild, sexy, and uninhibited, and needless to say, it produced a lot of attention.

The attention I began to receive was just what I needed to take my mind off the pains of life. As I stepped into this new identity, people treated me differently, and I welcomed it. I found myself getting involved in and agreeing to things I would have never admitted to had there been no witnesses around when they took place. Take, for instance, the night of the co-ed hotel birthday party (which I, of course, told my mom would be just girls), where a game of truth-or-dare turned into an all-out sexually-charged game of just dares. Announcing that I would never turn down a dare and being one of the few that were single at the party, I was given the most sexually-based dares, and I took on every one of them. Or should I say, everyone except the one that was even too gross for me, so I acted as if I did it to keep it cool. Finally, it came down to my last dare of the night, and I received the ultimate dare of them all: Strip. After accepting the challenge, I made a quick escape to the bathroom to think about what I was about to do for the guys who would be watching. Though I put on a big and bad front, the truth was that I was terrified. What if I didn't look right and they laughed at me? What if, at the last minute, I flaked and got the same reaction I did from Pressure a couple years ago? My heart began to race, and it was as if I could feel my blood rushing through my veins. My thoughts were speeding around my mind, as if it were a race track. *I thought, I can't do this. I can't subject myself to the possibility of embarrassment and shame. But wait ... I have to.* I had already laid claim to the fact that I would do anything; I couldn't back down now. A few splashes of water on my face, a minute of practice, and a good look at how my recently slimmed body looked in my matching purple bra and thongs gave me the confidence I needed to finally walk out into the living area of the suite, to the few guys awaiting the show they were promised. *Come on, girl. You got this,* I thought. Ignoring the fears and reservations screaming in my head, I went through with my dare, and to my surprise, they enjoyed every minute of it as they threw money at me. The song ended, and I felt as if I had proven who I was. Now I would finally be that girl everybody wanted. Little did I know, this would become my new identity and my way of solving just about every insecure or unpleasant emotion from here on out.

One of the members of my audience that night and the main cause for my anxiety was Music. My mind remained on him the entire time, as if I was dancing just for him. Wondering what he was thinking scared me senseless, but I went through with it because I had something to prove. When we met up again at school the next week, he told me how great of a job I had done, but it never went any further than that. We really were just friends, and that's how I thought it would always remain, but that's not what I wanted. It had been six years since I first laid puppy dog eyes on him, but I had never built the courage to tell him how I felt. After exposing myself at the party that night and now knowing what he thought of me — or, at least, my performance — I felt I had enough courage to finally let him know how I truly felt. Much to my surprise, he reciprocated interest in me. Though, in my eyes, I was nowhere near his level; not to mention, he was taken. He had a girlfriend he had been dating a little over a month, but I couldn't let that stand in the way of me finally being happy with the one guy I had been dreaming of being with for years. I was sure that becoming his girlfriend would erase every pain and fill my mind with all the goodness I had been desperate to feel since I was thirteen years old. He was going to be my escape, and I promised I would be whatever he wanted me to be for him. This was it; I was finally going to belong to someone who was going to see that I actually was worth it. Maybe he would even change my thoughts about myself. Yep … this is what I had been waiting for, and there was nothing that was going to bring me down off this high …

Or so I thought.

CHAPTER 3
Two Birds, One Stone

Two months had gone by since the day I confessed my feelings to Music, and I was impatiently awaiting the day when he would finally be mine. Though he expressed some of the same feelings for me, he wanted to make sure things were finished between him and his soon-to-be ex-girlfriend before he and I went too far. I couldn't even believe I was thinking of putting myself in this position again. I had told him about my first time having sex with Church, and Music promised me it wouldn't be like that with him because he would never do that to me.

Oh, was he right. He finally broke up with his girlfriend, and soon enough, we found ourselves in the perfect place with the perfect backdrop and the perfect scenario to finally have sex with each other for the first time. As scared as I was and as inexperienced as I felt, Music not only made sure I was relaxed, but he paid attention to and touched every area of my body, and I loved it. He had done this before, so he knew exactly what he was doing. From the very first time we had sex, I was addicted, hooked, bound, attached, and every other synonym for "obsessed" with him. At sixteen years old, I officially became sexually active, and it became my high and my escape; the way Music made me feel was almost magical. Repeatedly feeding my lust caused my morals, standards, and religious beliefs to be tossed out the window. But then again ... who needs them when you've found the one you're going to spend the rest of your life with, right? Obviously, we were only teenagers, but I knew what I felt was real, so what was the big deal?

Author's Love Note: Well, the "big deal" is that, unless a man and a woman have been joined together in marriage, there should be no sexual intercourse. Sounds a bit "old school," I know, but now I actually understand why this "rule" was set in place. When you have sex or make love to someone, you leave a piece of yourself with them, and they with you. As casual sex partners, this can pose major problems when or if you two were to go your separate ways. Feelings begin to grow; it's no longer just a "casual" thing; now it's personal. You can't think beyond the agreement the two of you made to just keep things simple. I've seen it all too many times before. It has happened to me as well, and trying to free your soul from the ties of another is one of those next to impossible feats. And just to add the cherry on top, more often than not, one person becomes tied quicker or more tightly than the other, and that makes for some crazy (and sometimes deadly) arguments, actions, and reactions like those you may have seen in certain movies. Though they may just be thrilling stories for the big screen, those types of people are real, and things like that happen pretty often in real life.

Do you mind if I go a bit deeper?

Your body is a sacred place that only one person should have access to. After you've slept with many people before the one you vow to spend the rest of your life with, by the time you reach that person, you have shared the most intimate parts of yourself that only they should have the pleasure of experiencing.

The Bible says it like this:

1 CORINTHIANS 6:12-20 (The Message) - There's more to sex than mere skin on skin. Sex is as much spiritual mystery as physical fact. As written in Scripture, "The

two become one." Since we want to become spiritually one with the Master, we must not pursue the kind of sex that avoids commitment and intimacy, leaving us more lonely than ever—the kind of sex that can never "become one." There is a sense in which sexual sins are different from all others. In sexual sin, we violate the sacredness of our own bodies, these bodies that were made for God-given and God-modeled love, for "becoming one" with another. Or didn't you realize that your body is a sacred place, the place of the Holy Spirit? Don't you see that you can't live however you please, squandering what God paid such a high price for? The physical part of you is not some piece of property belonging to the spiritual part of you. God owns the whole works. So let people see God in and through your body.

Never had I felt this way about someone, and that feeling only grew after the night when our bond was sealed for life ... by blood. Once we realized what had happened, there was an instant mutual understanding that the dynamics of our relationship had officially changed; we were now completely soul-tied.

Over the course of the next few months, our time together grew scarce with his focus being on college and working, while mine was on trying to make it through my senior year of high school. I had been so focused on my relationship, my image, and my sanity, that I had neglected my school work. So here I was at the end of the school year, trying to make up everything that I had neglected and missed. Never did I think that I would turn into that girl that made a guy and her image everything she cared about, but this relationship and this (seemingly) confident attitude now defined me. Nothing else mattered because I was determined to hold on to what was breathing life into me at the moment. For me, it was Music.

In May of 2003, the ninth cloud that I had been so carelessly riding on began to descend when the prom dress I had purchased just two months before fit a bit more snugly than I remembered. Come Monday morning, in the girls' bathroom, during my home economics class, I would find out why — I was pregnant. I pulled my best friend out of class, and she stood outside the bathroom stall, waiting for my response, as I was rendered speechless at the two bright pink lines that immediately showed up in the window on the stick. Even the dimly-lit, corner handicapped stall couldn't hide the truth. I couldn't even cry; I was in shock. She and I both were. My mind ran in a million different directions as I thought about all the things I loved to do now coming to a halt. If I was no longer be able to do any of those things, who would I be now? I slowly walked down the deserted hall and back to class to inform a few friends and my teacher, who had bought the test for me, after telling her how I had been feeling lately. After revealing the truth, they suggested I make a phone call to Music and let him know what I had just found out. With shaky hands, I dialed the number and dreadfully waited for him to answer, secretly hoping that he wouldn't. Unfortunately for me, he did answer, and it was time to tell him what I had just found out. There was a short pause as he was at a loss for words at first. Then he spoke, and while maintaining a cool head, he said we would figure this out. What he failed to realize was that I had already "figured it out" — I was going to have an abortion. There was no way I was going to ruin his life this way. In my mind, though I may have deserved this, he did not.

Much to my surprise, Music was totally against the entire idea. Was he crazy? I was only seventeen and still in high school, and he had just started college as a rising football star, and neither one of us had jobs that paid enough to support a baby. No excuse was good enough for him, though. He stuck to his argument that we were responsible for this baby and that we shouldn't seek the easy way out just because we had made a mistake. For an entire week, we argued back and forth until I finally told him the decision was ultimately mine, whether he agreed with it or not. I backed up my argument by reminding him that I wanted to attend college and reminding him of the disappointment that would come from our parents — mainly my church and family — and the fact that I did not want to become a statistic. He finally gave up. For the next couple of days, I heard nothing from Music until he showed up at my front door with information and papers to fill out. It was the paperwork from the abortion clinic. He walked in, tossed the papers at me, and walked back out. The glue that was holding my heart together cracked. Why was he so angry? Didn't he realize that I was doing us both a favor by not becoming the burden we really didn't need at that time? I still may not have known who I truly was, but one thing was for sure: I didn't want this to be the thing that defined me.

It was so hard to be in this position — too scared to tell anyone, all the while, trying to make the right decision for myself, this baby, and its father ... all at the same time. Every decision seemed like the right one, and every decision seemed like the wrong one. I secretly wished that there was someone I could share this secret with, someone who would be able to guide me in the best direction. Someone like my sisters or my mother. I felt alone, and Music, once again, was ignoring me. This just made the decision to abort an easier one; there was no way I was going to let this ruin us. Reading through the paperwork was one of the hardest things I've ever done in my life, and it literally made me sick. My body physically reacted to the emotional pain and stress I was feeling. There was nothing I could do about it, so I called

Music to let him know that we needed to make a trip to the emergency room.

Music sat with me in the cold, small room enclosed with curtains. There was no privacy, as the conversations between the doctors, nurses, and patients could be heard by anyone within earshot of your bed. They ran tests, they asked questions, they took blood ... and they called my mom. *"I'm sorry. We have to tell your mom because you're a minor."* That was the last line left ringing in my ears as the nurse walked out of the triage room, leaving the curtain pulled open just enough for me to witness my mother's whole world come crashing down in an instant. This was one moment I had hoped I would never have to disappoint her with, but here we were, and it was happening. The car ride home was silent. My mother literally said nothing to me until the next morning, as she drove me to school. She asked me a few questions, just to gain some understanding. When I revealed my plans to terminate my pregnancy and be done with this whole ordeal, she nearly jumped out of her seat. Needless to say, she told me that I would be putting an end to those plans. The argument I had given Music was the same argument I presented to her, but she wasn't hearing any of it.

Was this really going to happen? Was I really going to go through with this entire pregnancy and become a teenage mom? Immediately, I was introduced to the worse feeling of them all: Depression. This one was so much deeper, though. I could no longer see any good reason for my existence. I wanted to die.

On the night it became real, my emotions were so overwhelming. They gripped me in such a way that I could not even make a sound. As every negative thought individually spoke to me, I found myself walking from my room to the top of the stairs in the hall, stopping to look down once I got there. I wrapped my arms around my stomach (which had begun to grow) as I rocked back and forth, wondering what would happen if I rocked hard enough to fall. Snapped out of my trance by the sound of footsteps approaching, I quickly walked back to my room, fell onto my bed, and screamed into my pillow in the midst of the darkness. I felt so singled out in a world full of people who would all soon be witnesses to the disgrace I was carrying around.

A couple of weeks after that terrifying night, I found myself still thinking about going through with the abortion, even after my mother told me that she'd dreamed of me dying on the operating table. Great. Two birds, one stone. It didn't scare me, and I didn't flinch. Just a few days later, a close friend of the family came to visit one afternoon and informed me that God had shown her a vision of my lifeless body on a table. It was then that my mother revealed that I was pregnant and planning to abort. My mother and this family friend begged me to change my mind, begged me to see God was trying to save my life, and even after this mistake, they begged me to see that He still loved me and would help me. The emptiness I felt overrode their pleas. I didn't care about how anyone else felt because I knew the truth: I deserved the worst punishment for feeding into my lust so carelessly and for being so irresponsible. It was at that moment that my mother switched roles. My mother is a minister, and in that moment, I became a soul that needed saving from death. As soon as she shut the door to the bedroom, those two women walked around the bed and prayed. No, they didn't just pray; they went to *war* against the demons in my mind and commanded that every evil thought and feeling be evicted. As for me, I was lying on the floor in the midst of tears, depressing thoughts, and guilt, feeling as if I was getting weaker and weaker as the atmosphere seemed to become heavier and heavier. I had never experienced anything so powerful. After what felt like hours, they helped me up off the floor, and my mother wrapped me in her arms, reassuring me that everything would be all right. Though I still wasn't one hundred percent convinced, I made the decision to allow the little one that was growing inside of me to have a chance at experiencing life and, hopefully, becoming a better person than me. The word soon got out about my pregnancy, and after their initial shock wore off, I was surrounded by support from my family and friends. Many were obviously disappointed, but no one rejected me as I thought they would. However, it mattered not how much love and support I received because I was still seeing life through the eyes of a statistic, and I felt like a burden and an embarrassment.

Through all the thoughts that had been invading my mind for so long and now the shame of my pregnancy, I forgot to focus on school and found myself short a few credits by the time graduation came around. Here we go again. Devastation. Embarrassment. Hurt.

Confusion. Pain. All of that and more. At this point, my only choice was to make up the credits in summer school and graduate with the other seniors from every other school in the region who were facing the same fate. Having to graduate in the summertime with the rest of the "slackers" drove my sense of self-worth even lower. To add insult to injury, I also had to graduate with an obvious growing belly I was unable to hide, even with my oversized, shameful white gown (which would have been red had I graduated on time with my class). When graduation day finally came for me, though I smiled on the outside, I knew there was no real reason to celebrate, so I didn't. Why would we celebrate something that should have happened two months ago on the main stage room at Constitution Hall in Washington, D.C., instead of here, in a small school auditorium that couldn't even hold enough fold-out chairs to seat everyone's parents? Not only that, but was anyone looking at me? Surely, they were aware of the disgrace that was protruding from my then small-framed body, as I paraded across the small stage, at a ceremony that felt thrown together for a misfit. I simply could not understand the reason for their happiness or see the need for celebration. At least, there was no need to celebrate me. There was no reason to toss my undecorated cap, no reason to run and hug everyone, scream "We made it!", or fill the memory card on my camera with pictures from this day. When the ceremony ended, I walked to the back to find my family, and we snapped a few photos with me forcing out a smile through the tears that were preparing to avalanche from my eyes at any given moment. I had had enough of this day and wished that it would just end.

This shame I felt was carried all the way through to the birth of my daughter. Five months after graduating from high school, and only three weeks after my eighteenth birthday, I was lying in a hospital bed, staring at the beautiful, ebony-skinned princess beside me.

Instantly, I realized that, though I loved her because she was my own, I had no idea how to love her as a mother. I took care of her because she was mine, and I fed her from my breasts, but I found it hard to connect with her heart-to-heart. All I could think of was how adamant I had been about getting rid of her; I didn't even want her, but now she was here, and I didn't know how to handle it. There were times she would cry, and I would just look at her, paralyzed by fear and disbelief, which would result in a breakdown of my own emotions, with me crying right along with her. This was so unfair to such an innocent, perfect little girl, to be forced to have me as a mother. What had I done? I didn't know how to love her. Would she ever love me? She needed me, but could I provide for her with what she needed? When she got older, would she end up hating me for being an incompetent mother in the early stages of her life? Would I ever even learn how to be her mother?

Now introducing my newest friend: Doubt.

Just A Piece of Peace

Waiting for, hoping, expecting a changing

I'm speaking, but it's like you're not hearing me.

I'm thinking,

What's the point to this prayer thing,

If God doesn't even care? He

Sees me dealing with things I need healing from

Pains, old scars, and what I'll deal with tomorrow

Cuz see, it's like there's no ending to this thing

No freedom from this sorrow.

What's the point in waiting for nothing

To take you nowhere

And give you no relief?

What's the point of waiting

When it seems you can't even get a piece of peace?

CHAPTER 4
Identity Crisis

He asked, so I said yes. No, it may not have been the most romantic proposal or the best time, as I felt like I was twelve months pregnant, but I said yes. Okay, so I was only eighteen years old at the time and knew nothing about being a wife, but he meant more to me than I meant to myself. He gave me a reason to live, and if there was a way that I could keep that feeling around forever, I was going to do so. The question that loomed over the entire situation, however, was, why he ever asked me to begin with? I was so unstable in everything I did; I had even broken up with him twice already. My fear was that I wouldn't know how to turn off who I had been for so long, to become the wife he needed. I had no idea how to run a household, outside of what I had seen my mother do for years. How could he even trust me to be what he needed? Although I admit that the idea of planning a big, beautiful wedding and wearing a big, beautiful white dress sounded exciting to a young girl, I didn't really understand what I was getting myself into. Too afraid to voice my concerns, for fear of seeming as if I was rejecting him and letting everyone down, I decided to keep quiet and just go along with the whole thing.

Soon enough, however, in January of 2005, everything changed. We were set to be married in June, but the new year rolled in, our baby girl turned one year old, and my anxiety had grown to maximum capacity. I could no longer handle it; I didn't want to just go along with things anymore. Decisions were being made all around me, and every time I had to think about one thing, decide on another thing, and add this thing to that list, the stress grew more and more. At times, it became so overwhelming that I didn't know if I could bear it anymore. Though planning a wedding was a stressful process, my stress originated from the fact that I wasn't even sure this was what I really wanted. Things had begun to get harder between me and Music, and I felt like I had become forcefully strapped into a roller coaster ride that was set to one speed — too fast. I confided in my diary about how I didn't want to break his heart, but I didn't want him to marry me in the state I was in, or I would surely break it anyway. There was no way around it. He deserved better than this. He deserved better than *me*, so I found myself breaking things off once again, but this time, it hurt him a bit more.

The world seemed to stop the moment I told Music that I didn't want to go through with the wedding anymore. He reacted as if I didn't just call the wedding off, but as if our whole relationship had come to a halt as well. There was nothing he could do about it. If I didn't want to get married, it wasn't going to happen. He didn't agree, neither did he accept it, but my mind was made up, so everything was called off. The pressure of having to become a married woman so soon was now gone, but the pain of disappointing the love of my life far outweighed that. Over and over again, I tried to remind myself that what I was doing was a good thing, but with the way my mind was spinning and the painful look on his face every time he came over to pick up the baby, it made me feel otherwise. I felt so guilty. Music had injured himself while playing football in college. This ended his season and his college career. He was now working two jobs just to support us. So why couldn't I put my feelings aside for one moment to give him the happiness he obviously wanted and deserved? The time that was supposed to be taken to get myself together turned into a month-long debate between myself and I on whether or not I should just decide to go through with this wedding and learn as I go along. After all, was there really so much more to being married versus dating, besides living with each other?

Being faced with such a hard, life-changing decision at such a young age ... this felt like déjà vu. I was transported back to the time I had decided to have an abortion. The disappointment in the voices of those around me, coupled with the pain and disappointment on Music's face ... I knew I had to make things right. My feelings of doubt about being a good wife turned into fear. I was afraid I would lose the love and support of everyone. I worried that Music would move on and find real, mature love for himself. No one could fix this but me, and that was just what I decided to do.

I decided to meet up with Music to tell him that I had finally gotten a handle on things and that I was ready to take on the challenge of learning to be a wife. Yes, I lied. I did not have a handle on anything, and I was not ready to take on this challenge, but it was all I knew to do to put things back together. Therefore, I made the unhealthy decision to push past what I was truly feeling within myself and call the wedding back on. From that moment on, my life and the decisions I made in it were no longer my own. I needed to make sure that everyone was satisfied by my decisions from here on out.

A couple of nights before my wedding day, my girlfriends took me out to the nightclub for one last girls' night before I would be tied down forever. Finally able to take my mind off every feeling of doubt, fear, discomfort, and uncertainty, I danced the night away. The music from one of my favorite songs echoed throughout the room, and as I danced out to an open space on the floor, I got this feeling that there were eyes on me. After panning the room while continuing to dance, I looked over to the big window that overlooked the staircase leading down to the main level and realized that I was right. Why not indulge in a little fun? After all, this was my last time coming to the club as a single woman. I danced closer to the piercing stare from across the room, but the closer I got, the more I began to realize something. These eyes belonged to a female who, from across the room, very much resembled a male. As true as this was, much to my surprise, it didn't alter my reaction or my *attraction* to her. Continuing to dance, I enticed her and clearly captivated her, as she talked about me to a couple of guys with a smile on her face. At the end of the night, as I walked past her, she stopped me and gave her number to me ... and I took it. Something that I never thought I would do, that had never even crossed my mind, had now become a reality. Looking at her seductively, I let her know my interest had been peaked, and I made sure she watched me tuck her number into my bra just before I slowly walked away and down the stairs with my girls. Little did I know, I had just opened myself up to a whole new set of mind games and emotional confusion, but I would soon find out.

Finally, it was a beautiful Saturday in August — a perfect setting for a wedding — and with the secrets of what took place a couple of nights before hidden away, I prepared myself to become a married woman. My fear became hidden by the excitement of the day, by the smiles of my family, and the thought of my fiancé awaiting his beautifully painted bride to walk down the aisle all dressed in white (a color she was not worthy to wear). Just as I stepped behind the closed double doors in the back of the church that led to the sanctuary where I would stand before God and man and make the biggest commitment of my life, I began to shake uncontrollably. My mother was doing me the honor of walking me down the aisle, and as we linked arms, she noticed my sudden hesitation, looked at me, and asked if I was ready. Within my mind, a million NOs screamed out; instead, a quiet yes escaped my lips. The doors opened, and just as my sister was about to sing, I froze. *"Wait!"* I was petrified. The doors closed again, and I began to breathe heavily as the wedding planner fanned my face to dry up my impending tears. Little did she and my mom know, those were tears of terror because this little bird was not ready to fly. They both assured me that I would be fine, that this part would be over soon, and I would be so happy. Although I wasn't so sure how true their statements were, this was happening, so I took a few deep breaths, put on my happy face, said, "Okay, I'm ready," and walked down the aisle. Yes ... I lied again.

The words "I do" changed my entire life within one split second. A question mark had replaced the period behind what should have been a confident statement, causing the very meaning to switch from a declaration to uncertainty. I had officially allowed everyone in my life to decide my future, alter my judgment, and become lords over my heart and mind.

Author's Love Note: Too many times, I've heard people say, "You're my reason for living," or "You complete me," to their parents, spouses, or children. It is a beautiful thing to love someone with such a deep love that they become irreplaceable in your life, but when you say you are not a complete person without them or you make them your reason for everything, you begin to make them your god.

You must understand that people are nothing but mere flesh and bone and capable of failure. To put all of your hope, all of your trust, all of your dependence on flawed beings will create a life full of pain and disappointments for you. Your trust, hope, reliance, surety, and confidence should be in God alone.

The Bible says it like this:

Psalm 118:8-9 (NLT)

8 "It is better to take refuge in the Lord

than to trust in people.

9 It is better to take refuge in the Lord

than to trust in princes."

Isaiah 2:22 (NIV)

22 Stop trusting in mere humans, who have but a breath in their nostrils.

Why hold them in esteem?

Jeremiah 17:5-8 (NLT)

5 This is what the Lord says:

"Cursed are those who put their trust in mere humans,

who rely on human strength

and turn their hearts away from the Lord.

6 They are like stunted shrubs in the desert,

with no hope for the future.

They will live in the barren wilderness,

in an uninhabited salty land.

7 "But blessed are those who trust in the Lord

and have made the Lord their hope and confidence.

8 They are like trees planted along a riverbank,

with roots that reach deep into the water.

Such trees are not bothered by the heat

or worried by long months of drought.

Their leaves stay green,

and they never stop producing fruit.

Why I decided to take the route of verses dealing with trusting God, instead of man, is because, during these times in my life, I put all my trust, confidence, hope, and assurance in my family and my fiancé. I trusted them to be the ones to validate me. I trusted them to be the ones to keep my happiness at its height. I trusted them to be the ones to keep me overflowing with love, instead of remembering that God is love. I took my eyes off what God said he could and would do for me, and everything he said that he is, and I focused on human ability alone. I even put my trust in myself by thinking I was making the right decision by overlooking how I felt and believing that it would be all right. At least, I would have everyone on my side to hold me up should I feel down or fall. This is not the way we should think or live.

God, being the only one who knows your end from your beginning, who knew you before He formed you in your mother's womb, is the only one in whom such a reliance should be. Trust God to make you feel better about yourself and whatever situation lies before you. Be warned: If you continue to make people your reason, your answer, your comfort, or your hope and peace, you will find yourself in a worse position emotionally, compromising in certain areas and doing things you thought you never would to maintain happiness.

Ask me how I know.

A few weeks after being wed in holy matrimony, the realization of what I had done — that I had become a wife — hit me hard. The depression and anxiety I had tried so hard to mask and fight against over the past few months, strongly showed themselves once again. Nothing satisfied me anymore, not even God or my new husband. Desperate to escape reality, I searched for an out, something that would take my mind off my reality. It wasn't long before I put the titles of *mom* and *wife* to the side. Partying, drinking, and getting high became my norm. There were times when Music would come with me, but because I saw him as the chains that kept me locked within the confines of what felt like a prison, I often went without him. Soon enough, however, even living wild and free like I did at sixteen was no longer satisfying me. I felt stuck. Unfulfilled. Unprepared. Unhappy. I hated myself because I had ignored every sign that told me I wasn't ready for this, all for the sake of pleasing people.

About a month before our wedding, the apartment we had planned to move into fell through, leaving us no choice but to move in with my new husband's family once we returned from our honeymoon. This was not how I imagined the start of my marriage would go. As I was going through my boxes one afternoon, I came across the balled-up piece of napkin with the name and number of the girl I had met at the club faded into it. I didn't even know I still had it; I had thought nothing of it until then. At that moment, however, curiosity didn't just set in; it took over. I gave in. Dialing her number was what drove me across the line into a world I never knew would consume me the way it was going to. She was surprised to hear from me (I was just as surprised as she was), but she expressed how much she looked forward to meeting up with me. Yeah ...

we made those plans. I began to see this girl regularly, and it opened me up deeper and wider to lust. I would sneak off to go be with her, or even let my husband know where I was going and with whom, without letting him in on the secret that she was a lesbian and that we were involved with each other. Being with her changed me in a way I hadn't felt in a long time; I found myself craving her. When we were together, she gave me those butterflies I had stopped feeling from Music. I would go to her house, or we would touch and kiss on each other in the back of my car; with her, I was uninhibited. There was one problem, however ... being with her, or even sometimes thinking about being with her sexually, made me feel ... disgusted. I was so confused, but I kept up the charade and fed my corrupted flesh the temporary, unfulfilling meal of being with this girl over and over again.

Over the course of the next couple of months, I noticed that my sexual desires began to not only change but grow. I found myself becoming involved in and sitting in the midst of all types of sexually-charged atmospheres. There were times I would be sitting in the same room with two or a few other people who were either having intercourse or performing oral sex on each other, and it didn't seem to bother me. My mind had become perverted, and I had become very open to all things sexual, and had even tried my hand at a few new things when my curiosity got the best of me.

Yep ... been there, done that ... and that.

Confessions

I must confess. Sometimes I envy the world,

A foolish girl to envy the world

But in times like these, the world seems to have the best solutions,

Resolutions to life and all of its negative contributions

To my evolution from girl to woman.

Challenges keep comin; hurdles keep me jumpin'

Over and over can't keep up; my strength's not enough.

That's why I turned to you, GOD,

But that's when life became hard.

Can't solve problems like I used to.

Now I must trust in you.

"Be not conformed to this world"; no longer a naive girl

But trapped inside, the world's still alive,

And all this time, I thought it died,

But it's not dead, just minimized,

Hidden from untrained eyes

Much to my surprise, when it began to rise, I welcomed it with open arms

Thinking it could do no harm.

But lookie, lookie, she's still a rookie

Got this world teasing me

The very thing that's pleasing me.

But in my mind, I make it right,

Saying, "Lord, it would be so nice, if only for one night.

Let this be my place of peace."

From place of peace, to want and need

Now I'm in too deep ...

Soon enough, I found myself eyeing other girls, one being someone I worked with. Seeing her five days a week only caused my interest to grow. Knowing that I was attracted to her, she would say things as I walked past her cubicle and would stare me down as she slowly made her way past mine. She was toying with me, wanting to see just how far she could take me. After working late one Friday afternoon, as I was leaving the office, I noticed she had missed the bus, so I offered her a ride to the train station. The conversation in the car began casually, but it soon made a sharp turn, the more comfortable we became with each other. Before I knew it, I had driven all the way to my neighborhood. I told her that I would simply take her to the station near me, unless she had another suggestion. *Bird, what are you doing?* After talking for a few more minutes, we both decided that it probably wouldn't be a good idea to take things too far, for fear of our working relationship becoming strained. She also knew that I was married, and she expressed that, though she may have flirted with me in the office, she would never step in the middle of a relationship between a husband and a wife. When we arrived at the station, she kissed my hand and waved good-bye until next week. I couldn't help but smile the whole way home, as my stomach fluttered uncontrollably.

What was happening to me? Did I forget that I was married? And as a Christian, I was not supposed to take part in a lesbian lifestyle? Secretly, I didn't really want to entertain the idea of being with another woman, so what was going on? Something wasn't adding up, and realizing that I was getting out of control, I decided to pray. I had gotten caught up, but I always knew where I could go for answers. My relationship with God may not have been the best or the strongest, but I had grown up with the understanding that, if you got to that place where you'd tried everything, and everything had failed, try Jesus. As I sat quietly in my room that evening, it hit me. The very idea of being with an actual woman was what turned me off. I had even tried to flirt with a "girly" girl once before, and though she flirted back, I wasn't turned on. Any female that actually caught my attention looked like a male, but I knew I wasn't attracted to her. I was attracted to the guy she looked like, but I appreciated the attention I received from her. Although these girls lived their lives looking like men, they knew exactly what I, as another woman, wanted to hear or feel while in their presence, and that was what kept my attention. I was not bi-sexual or a lesbian; I simply wanted attention, and it became more and more clear as time went on.

It was time to put an end to this entire thought in my mind. First decision: Stop seeing the girl from the club. I went to her house and explained to her that I didn't want to live this double life anymore. I didn't condemn her for her lifestyle choices, but I told her that, not only did I want to stop being secretive around my husband, but I had never even had an interest in exploring this world — the world she lived in — which she surprisingly understood. I walked away from her feeling happy and free, believing that I was now in a good place, but God took it a whole step further. The girl that I had been flirting with at my job was still around. How was I supposed to ignore her? There were days where I just couldn't fight it, and it began to eat at me. Not more than two weeks later, a new manager came into the office and began to shake things up. Before I knew it, I was being called into her office to speak with her and my supervisor about my employment status. My attendance had been great, my personality was loveable, and my performance was a force to be reckoned with since I had started eight months ago, so what was the problem? As it would turn out, I was let go due to something so small, something I (and a few other employees) had been doing since being hired, something my supervisor said was okay to do, yet denied it to the boss. I could not believe this was happening to me; I was devastated. After some time went by, I finally realized what had taken place. The lesson that came out of this was hard, but I had asked God for help with breaking away from this girl, and he did just that. That day, though the circumstances were not favorable, I was able to walk out of that office, and just like that, she was out of my life for good.

CHAPTER 5
Emotional Rollercoaster

Growing up, my mother was always traveling from place to place, preaching and teaching the Gospel, and I always traveled with her. I witnessed so many people's lives being changed both from the words she spoke and from countless other preachers and teachers who stood in the pulpit ministering. Though I loved church, sometimes I would come to my own conclusions about the things that took place from watching church people and their shenanigans. At times, this made it hard to believe in, or even want to experience, the power of God for myself. Between preachers pushing and slapping people on the forehead and people falling out on the floor, shaking and screaming ... sometimes I just didn't know how to handle it all.

It wasn't until April 2006 (the same month I was fired from my job), when my godsister and I traveled with my mother down to Wilmington, North Carolina, that I experienced something I will never forget for the rest of my life. She was going to preach, and it felt no different from any other time until that evening at the youth service. My mother is an evangelist, a lover of people, a servant, and an awesome speaker who has always inspired me, but this night, she spoke a message that pierced me to my soul. Maybe it was because I was so vulnerable. Maybe it was the Spirit of God that was in the church from the beginning of the service. Maybe it was the fire that she preached with. Maybe I really did want and expect God to touch me. Maybe it was all of the above. Whatever it was, one thing I know for certain, I was forever changed from that one night. She called all the youth that were in the building to come up to the front of the church. We all flooded the front, kneeled at the altar, and cried out to God. All of a sudden, I felt what can only be described as a hot wind blow over each of us, and one by one, we became touched by the Spirit of God and began to speak in tongues. The amazing thing was that I wasn't the only one who had experienced this wind, as my mother and some of the other teens expressed what they felt as well. That night, I knew for sure I was changed completely and that I could finally be all that I needed to be for my husband, my daughter, and God.

I was in a total euphoric state and excited to return home to share with Music everything that had happened and how different things were going to be. One thing that I totally forgot — or didn't really understand at the time — was what my grandmother had always told me. She always said, *"The closer you get to God, the harder the devil will fight you, so be prepared."* Over the next few years, I found this out first-hand.

After hearing about my experience and witnessing the changes that took place within me soon after, Music made the decision to dedicate his life to God as well. This was the best decision we had ever made for ourselves and each other; I felt like everything was finally going to be the way I had always imagined. We were fighting less, and I was even smiling more. For a while, everything was perfect; I had a new job, and a new car. Things were going well for us, yet the feeling remained. Something was missing. Since deciding to live right and depend on God more, I stopped doing everything and going everywhere that I once did for fun. The mistake that I made was not finding something else (more productive) to replace my time and energy with. Once again, I became bored, unsatisfied, and frustrated, this time, to the point of anger. Everything Music tried to do for me failed because I was so consumed with myself and my feelings that I didn't know how to receive any kind of love from him. There were times he would upset me to the point where I wouldn't speak to him for days, and I found it harder and harder to connect with my baby girl on a mother-daughter level because, truth be told, I didn't want to be in that situation. My anger, once again, reared its ugly head, and I began to say and do things in a fit of rage that were unthinkable, like physically taking it out on Music. Trying to restrain me, hold me down, or push me away didn't always work, so he fought back. We were still living with his parents at the time and finally got caught fighting when his mother came downstairs one evening to see what the commotion was about. While she yelled at the both of us, I pushed Music away, ran up the stairs, and out the front door to my car. He came after me, but once he got within arm's reach, I pushed him again. What happened next was a blur, since all I can recall were my glasses flying into the air and landing in the grass. Clearly, this wasn't his intention as he immediately tried to grab me and apologize for what he had just done, but I was too erratic to listen. Blinded by tears, I searched through the grass and quickly found my glasses. I threw them on my face, jumped in my car, and drove off with Music banging on the window, screaming, "Please get out the car!"

He wanted to talk to me reasonably, but my mind was too far gone to even be rational at that moment. I took with me no thoughts about my baby girl. I had no idea where I was going. I had no license, no money, and no clothes in case I decided to stay wherever I ended up. My disappointment with the way that I had allowed things to turn out for myself was driving me mad.

There was no way that this was my life; there was no way I was going to be stuck like this forever. Where was the happiness? The peace? The satisfaction? Though I had no plans to physically leave my marriage, there was no way I was going to remain unsatisfied while I stayed in it. My first thought was not the arms of another man; however, that's ultimately where I ended up. It fed my desire and cured the unsatisfactory feeling, in addition to getting high. I knew what I was doing and feeling wasn't right, and in my heart, I sincerely wanted to fix it, but there was one problem: I was trying to do it alone. Of course, I never told Music about how I was feeling and the actions it led to, and I was much too worried about how crazy and unstable I would sound to anyone else, so I decided to keep silent about the fight that was taking place within me. Bad decision. I tried to correct my actions by myself and fight the way I felt. Taking on different hobbies and activities to cure my boredom seemed to work for a little while, but whenever a problem arose at home, anger struck me, and I got off course once again.

I started getting high more frequently, even begged friends to blow the smoke in my face, desperate for the carefree feeling that I knew would follow after just a few pulls from a blunt or simple contact. In the beginning, Music was aware of what I was doing, as we would get high with friends together. However, when he became uninterested in it, I would sneak off to experience this seventh heaven and blow away the stress life brought about daily. Yes, I understood what I was doing wasn't good for me, but I was so unhappy, and I felt so lifeless that, if anything was going to give me wings, I was going to take it. The party life became my life, and I often found myself hanging out with my single friends, indulging in the "freedom" they had. Though I continued to fulfil my obligations as a wife and a mother, my mind wasn't at home, and it showed. There were times I tried to fight against my thoughts and settle myself, but that seemed like a daily uphill, losing battle, which was stressful. End result: Closet. Freakum dress. Time to party. This became my new secret identity. Not even Music knew who I was at times.

In the midst of all of this, I unintentionally reconnected with a guy I knew named Bass and began talking to him regularly. As it would turn out, Bass catered to the part of me that I felt Music did not. It wasn't a physical attraction, but his words and acts of kindness melted me over time. Finally, he asked me out to dinner, and though I was reluctant at first, I ended up very happy that I had said yes. I was wined and dined, cared for, treated delicately, and kissed sweetly. Bass treated me like a lady, and for almost a month, I indulged in all of it, as it was feeding the need to be desired. It was all "innocent" fun until we were snapped back to reality one evening when we thought someone was after us. I had agreed to go back to his place late one evening, knowing that I didn't really want to be there. There was no legitimate reason as to why I said yes, except that I didn't want to make him upset or sound scared and insecure. Sound familiar? We did not have sex, but we were in his bedroom when a suspicious noise came from the living room of his small apartment. It sounded as if someone was sneaking around. He jumped up to go check things out, and although he reassured me that I was protected, I prayed and told God that, if He got me out of there, I would end this whole relationship and never come back. After cautiously walking around, making sure everything was clear, he decided to take me back home, just to be safe. A bit shaken up, but happy, I quickly grabbed my things and rode back home, relieved that I was safe, but more so that God had helped me escape once again. Over time, our conversations became fewer and further between until they stopped completely. God answered my prayer that night, so I made good on my promise to Him.

Things got better – once again – for a period of time. I was maturing, and we were growing stronger in our faith. The three of us were getting closer as a family. I had another new (better) job, and we were finally looking to move into our own apartment. It seemed as if everything was falling right into place ... until a few months after the move. It didn't take long for me to realize that moving out was only a portion of what I really needed to be happy. The company I was working for filed for bankrupcy, so I lost my job. Our daughter was now in school, and Music worked crazy hours, so most of the day, I sat at home alone, feeling purposeless. I had recently made the decision not to get high anymore, which meant dealing with my reality without an escape. Writing soon became my escape and gave me a different type of high, but it didn't solve my need for satisfaction or the lack of excitement at home. Music and I had days and months filled with happy times that I wished would never end, but I couldn't quite shake the nagging feeling that I needed something more than this.

In 2008, I was formally introduced to a man I had only remembered meeting a couple of times before: Mister. After a meeting one evening, we sat and talked casually, but suddenly I felt compelled to let him into my world of lack of excitement and boredom at home. He gave me no reason to feel like I could be this open with him, but once I started, I just couldn't stop. The need and the desire to talk to someone with an unbiased opinion was so strong, and he seemed like the perfect person to pour out to. After a short while, what seemed harmless in the beginning took on a whole different identity. Knowing in my mind I needed to get back to Music, we still talked for hours that evening, exchanging stories about our home lives, and found that we had a bit more in common than we thought. Never in a million years did I think I would be talking this way to someone like him, someone on his level. He found it to be shocking as well, how I could captivate him like this. Little did we know, this was the beginning of a secret relationship that would be founded on reckless emotions and evolve into a deep lust for one another.

[UNTITLED]

What am I doing?

What am I feeling?

What am I expecting?

Why am I tripping?

My mind spinning, like I'm sippin' on gin and juice

Got me twisted

Drunk off everything that is you

How you do what you do and all you produce

High off a fantasy that's coming to reality

Now sits as a memory ...

How could this be?

When did it happen?

From teacher to friend to the center of my attraction

My distraction

Not from duties, but from all that I'm lacking,

It's fascinating how you can make me go crazy.

Just from hearing you speak, it makes me weak,

Sends chills up my spine, the thought of you being mine.

Just one time to feel like you were my man

Man ...

See what I mean?

You got me feeling this way I don't understand.

I can't deny it, and I won't fight it

Cuz, to be totally honest ... I like it.

- September 14, 2009 (edited for content discretion)

There was this unspoken passion between us that I realized I didn't share with Music anymore. A simple text or even an e-mail would make me radiate with desire and cause me to anxiously sit and wait for his responses to my flirtatious messages. Business was no longer just business, it became a way to keep the sexually-charged communication flowing between us. Days turned into weeks, weeks turned into months, emotions turned into sexual attraction and late-night intimate phone calls where I allowed his voice to calm the raging storm that brewed on the inside of me. In return, I provided him with the words he needed to allow his imagination to run wild, giving him the release he had been desperate for. This, I thought for certain, was Music's fault; he was the one not taking care of what belonged to him. If he had an understanding of how to satisfy someone like me, then I wouldn't have the urge to fall into the waiting arms of other men ... right?

Author's Love Note:

Psalm 37:4-6 (NLT)

4 Take delight in the Lord,

and he will give you your heart's desires.

5 Commit everything you do to the Lord.

Trust him, and he will help you.

6 He will make your innocence radiate like the dawn,

and the justice of your cause will shine like the noonday sun.

For those of you who have felt, thought, or are thinking the way I was in this portion of my story, I want you to understand that the problem is not your spouse. The problem is you. Whether you are male or female, old or young, if you are the one dealing with deep-seated issues, then the problem has never been them; it has always been you.

Sounds pretty harsh, but let me explain.

When you come to this point, as I did, you begin to subconsciously look for things and reasons that support your argument. Something as normal as the way they brush their teeth becomes annoying or you aren't satisfied even when they complete the tasks you asked them to complete. Yes, I have been there! The problem lies in the fact that you are, once again, depending on human flesh to satisfy and complete you. Now please don't get me wrong and think I am saying your spouse is not supposed to satisfy you because we are made to come together for flesh on flesh satisfaction. There are actual parts of the male and female anatomy in which their design and purpose are purely for sexual satisfaction. For any relationship to remain healthy, it's imperative that both individuals remain attentive to the other's emotional needs and desires. Staying in communication with each other is the best way to reassure that this happens. However, those are your feelings or emotions, but what I am speaking of is your SOUL. This type of satisfaction will only come from God. Yes, you can create happy moments with people, but only God can bring you complete joy and satisfy your soul.

Psalm 16:11 (KJV)

11 Thou wilt shew me the path of life: in thy presence is fulness of joy; at thy right hand there are pleasures for evermore.

Psalm 107:8-9 (KJV)

8 Oh that men would praise the Lord for his goodness, and for his wonderful works to the children of men!
9 For he satisfieth the longing soul, and filleth the hungry soul with goodness.

I was searching for satisfaction, but what I didn't realize was that only Jesus would be able to quench that thirst, that hunger that I had for so much more.

John 6:35 (NLT)

Jesus replied, "I am the bread of life. Whoever comes to me will never be hungry again. Whoever believes in me will never be thirsty.

There may be those of you that are reading this book that are looking for satisfaction in some or many areas of your life. Realize that it is not always an "at home" issue. I was bored with life and unsatisfied with the way things were turning out; I felt unproductive and useless in the small things I was doing. This had nothing to do with my husband, but because he was the one I depended on to satisfy my human nature, it all fell on him. Until you learn how to find happiness within yourself, you will never be able to experience complete satisfaction or even fullness of joy. The Bible makes this clear, but don't take it as a threat or a curse. Take it as direction from a loving God who knows that man will fail you. Therefore, He would rather you put all of your trust, hope, confidence, and dependence in Him, so He can make sure you will be satisfied from your head to your soul.

Our relationship had developed into something that ran deeper than what we shared with our spouses. This wasn't about love or even lust, this was about our connection. The day came where the opportunity to be alone presented itself. We tried to play it cool by keeping things strictly business, but when our eyes locked, I found myself pouncing on him like a lioness capturing her prey. This was wrong ... this was so wrong because we were both married. Though it took a few more seconds, I finally pushed away from him, causing him to fall back into his chair. With my heart racing, I slowly walked away to go collect my thoughts on what had just taken place. My emotions were going awry, and when he walked over to check on me, it happened again. This was wrong ... this was so wrong. Before getting into a position that we both knew we wouldn't be able to get out of, I put a stop to it again. My conscience became louder than the screaming desire to give into the temptation that stood before me.

What kept drawing me to him was how he made me feel. Yes, he was very attractive, but the boldness I felt to just be myself around him — and sometimes the vixen I imagined myself to be — was what really turned me on.

I needed this; I didn't want to go back to being insecure, fake, and unstable. Being in this secret relationship caused creativity to pour out of me. He became my muse for some very erotic short stories that I wrote whenever I needed to get away from reality. But this was wrong ... this was so wrong. Never had I ever even thought of stepping out with a married man. Although he was already unhappy at home, I felt like a homewrecker. I had become the "other woman," and neither the thought nor the title was one I wanted to have. The thought of this same thing happening to Music — some young chick throwing herself at him — made me both scared and furious, to the point where thoughts and ideas compiled into a form of reality in my mind. All from my imagination, I began to walk around the house angry, making small comments concerning him seeing other women, and it caused even more of a rift between us. I was the one who had been unfaithful, but I dragged my husband's image through the mud in my mind, convincing myself that he, too, was up to no good.

It took quite some time to sever this affair with Mister (over a year to be exact), but I finally made the decision to let him go. I was not in love with him, and I knew I did not want a life with him, but the way I felt when I was with him was powerful and hard to simply throw away. As hard as it was, however, my relationship with Music and my fear of God rang louder in my ears, louder than my desires to be (emotionally) satisfied by another man.

Over the course of the next few months, I didn't realize just how unsettled I was until a skit set to a song I was performing one evening became all too real. Acting has always been one of my favorite things to do (go figure), so I eventually auditioned for and became a member of an awesome Christian drama group. This group pulled out some of my deepest emotions, from practice nights and Bible studies to live performances. For this skit, the members of our group played demons dressed in all black, and as the man on the track sang about fighting the demons of your mind, they attacked me all at once. They pushed me down to the ground, pulled my hair, screamed, and growled in my face, laughing at me. It was definitely one of our more physical dramas. At the end of the skit, one of the guys who played the part of Jesus came in and rescued me from the demons and released me from the chains they had bound me with. Once released, we walked down the steps of the stage together, marking my freedom. What was taking place in my mind, however, was not in sync with what everyone was witnessing within the drama at the moment. After walking across the front of the sanctuary and through the double doors, I fell apart in his arms, feeling as if I had just been in a war. While the audience applauded what they believed to be good acting, he realized something wasn't right. Bursting through the doors of the room where we all had been preparing before the service, he turned me over into the hands of our group mother, who immediately sensed what I was dealing with. My anger rose to such a point that they had never seen before, so she prayed, telling me to fight and stop giving in. Her insight was always on target, and after a few more words of tough love, I broke down. My secrets were being exposed, and I just didn't know how to handle it.

The pain, embarrassment, and anger I felt that day played over and over in my head for a long time. Though I tried to fight it, I eventually gave into the fight I was obviously losing, and it took me to a point of no return. I couldn't take being unhappy another minute. I hated my job, my car had broken down, and the one we were given was worse, finances were getting harder to manage, church was becoming too much, and I couldn't keep up with the lifestyles my few friends seemed to be thriving in. The way I was feeling was not totally Music's fault, but I still blamed him for the angry, frustrated, unsatisfied person I had become. I had come to the part of the drama where I could choose to remain unhappy while hiding behind different masks and identities or exit stage left. I decided that it was time to end the façade; it was time for the curtain to close. This time, however, Music would eventually make the same decision to end this show.

CHAPTER 6
Soul Tied

Work it out is what they always say,

But what happens when "work it out" don't work

And we go our separate ways?

When the problems ain't solved

And the love don't flow

And the anger don't dissolve

Like salt in a cup of water, minus the H2O?

What then? What next?

How do we fix what's broken with no material left

To work with?

Why have we lost what we used to have and

Now every happy moment has turned to anger and sadness?

Days without rest, sleepless nights

Prolonged silence, meaningless fights.

When the focus from the both of us is to blame the other,

How do we take what's wrong and make it right?

The last few months of 2011 were, by far, the hardest and most liberating months I'd ever lived through to date. Though it seemed as if those two descriptions could never coincide with each other, with the events that took place and the mindset I had fallen into, it made perfect sense. I was tired, unsatisfied with life, unhappy at home, and I no longer cared to hide it or fight it. With Music and I on opposite ends of the boxing ring in the final round, it wouldn't be long before one of us was knocked out. The distance and tension between us caused things within our household to get so bad that we now had to make the decision to let our place go. We hadn't been working as a team, and that meant making unwise financial decisions, without a thought of the consequences. The freedom that we had finally gained after living with his family for the first three years of our marriage was snatched away in an instant. We found ourselves now living in my old bedroom in my mother's house, and all because we could not and *would* not come up with a plan together. After the move, things took a turn for the worse. Of all the times we had ever had a serious talk, we finally sat down and had the most serious one of them all: To stay or not to stay? That was the question. Not a question of remaining situated in my mother's house, but a question of would we stay there together. His parents' house was a seven-minute drive away, and the invitation for him (from them) to go back home was always open. There had been times where we both became so upset with each other and our entire situation that one of us would leave home for a night, but we would always come back. This time, we were talking something a bit more permanent — no coming back. As far as I was concerned, it was ultimately his decision to be made because mentally I had already packed my bags and checked out a long time ago.

The happy moments at home became fewer and further between and eventually drove me to the point of no return. Once again, I found myself wanting and eventually searching for something more to satisfy me. This time, I had begun to intentionally search for a man to fill that place of un-satisfaction, though I lived in denial. That denial began to fade when my satisfaction finally came. It slipped its way in, by showing up in the form of my long-lost, childhood crush Skillz; he contacted me through social media a few months before the move. *"You still married?"* was the question I was presented with after we hadn't spoken in years. We had a lot of catching up to do, though he had obviously already seen or read a few things I had shared. The start of this felt just like any of the other short-term, emotional interests I had stumbled into. The only difference was, with him, he wasn't exactly as sweet or even as captivated by me as the others were. He was straightforward, blunt, direct; he didn't beat around the bush. Honestly, he was one step away from obnoxious. Being on the receiving end of his un-sweetened, sometimes tasteless words, one would think that I would have run away, but I found myself intrigued, becoming a little too honest with him, hinting at the fact that I was bored at home. However, for the sake of saying I did so, I constantly defended the fact that I was still married and not looking for any type of outside entertainment, when I sensed the "harmless" flirting becoming a bit more prevalent. No matter how much I denied it, however, my marriage was ending. I was desperately seeking entertainment, and our frequent, flirtatious conversations were satisfying to me for the time being. Skillz and I kept in touch with each other, and by the end of the year, the exchange of words between us had become unrestricted. He became the break I looked forward to during my long work days.

When the opportunity to see him finally presented itself, I welcomed it with open arms and anticipation. I invited him to hang out, along with some family and friends for my birthday, and it turned into a night of so much more than I had ever expected. It had been about ten years since we were even in the same room, but the minute I saw him, the attraction was high, and the flirting was now obvious and shameless. Music also showed up that night because, after all, it was his "wife's" birthday that was being celebrated. Although I had let him know my plans for the night, I didn't really want him there, but obviously, I couldn't stop him if he wanted to be there. What an invitation, right? Even with Music in the room, the interaction between Skillz and I didn't stop. I was relentless and reckless, and I was loving every minute of his attention. A simple crush as a child had developed into a full-blown, adult, physical desire, and the sexual tension between the two of us grew by the minute. By the end of night, none of us were ready for it to end, so we decided to keep the party going elsewhere. Music reluctantly went home, leaving me behind, so an even greater sense of freedom came over me. The question was, however, what exactly did I want to do with that freedom? In just a few hours, I would find out. Though the thought had crossed my mind a hundred times before, I never really thought I would ever act on it. That night and into the early morning, however, that was exactly what I did. What I didn't realize until much later was that I had given Skillz more than just my body that night; I had given him my soul. Before we even got to the point of having sex, I connected with him on a level that I had not connected with Music in a long time. He made me laugh. He was witty (and rude), and he was just the right amount of "bad boy" with his roots in the church. He was creative and showed an interest in my creative side. He was unbridled, and he wanted me just as bad as I wanted him, or so I thought. From that night through the end of the week, I was living the life I had been desiring for years. Skillz was everything I had told Music that he was not.

We were uninhibited. We danced in the middle of the convenience store and bought as much junk food as we wanted. We had sex. We drove into the sunrise. We went shopping. We had sex. We sang and laughed at the top of our lungs, and we had sex. Skillz even reintroduced me to my love of getting high. Though I knew this was no good for me, I felt like myself with him. He truly was everything I had been missing. You would think that this part of my story would have been more toward the beginning, at least, before the experience I had at the youth service in North Carolina, but no. I had become the "saved on Sunday" Christian that non-believers (and believers alike) always ridicule and mock. However, I had become so unsatisfied in every other area of my life that I justified my actions and convinced myself that this was exactly the change I needed to finally be all right.

Wrong.

I had been touched by God but was running in the opposite direction. I was filled with lust, and Skillz satisfied it by providing me with everything (more than sex) that I had been denying or depriving myself of for years. Whenever I was with him, I said whatever I wanted to say. I was able to free myself and be whomever I wanted to be. It wasn't a fantasy like I had created with Mister. This was real. I became a master of deception as I came up with different reasons and excuses to tell my mother and my husband for why I was never home, and whether they believed them or not, I got away with it. My mind became so warped that I had completely lost sight of reality. The conversations between Skillz and I turned into what-ifs and possibilities of staying together; I was definitely soul-tied to him, and little did I know, it would turn out to be completely one-sided.

<u>*Author's Love Note:*</u> *It doesn't matter how "deep" you are or how close to God you are or not, understand that soul ties are one hundred percent REAL. It is absolutely imperative that you not only know who you're dealing with in a sexual partner but to also know what you are dealing with within yourself. If you are weak in any area, it is a perfect door for the enemy to walk right in and make himself at home. That is a big reason why it is taught to wait until marriage before you have sex with someone. Most times, you don't really find out about what a person is dealing with until you have been with them for a period of time, and the road to marriage tends to bring many things to the surface. A few chapters back, I said one of the consequences of sexually bonding yourself to someone*

other than your spouse is that, oftentimes, one person becomes more tightly bonded than the other.

I was that person.

I was the one who was searching for something. I was the one who was broken, in pain, in need and lonely, but I had masked it for so long and become so angry and desperate that I didn't even realize it. This is a dangerous place to be in, when you are an emotional wreck, even if it's not from relationship issues. Allowing someone to penetrate the most intimate parts of you will bring confusion to your heart and mind. Are you truly in love, or are those areas within you that haven't been touched or satisfied in a long time receiving the attention they've so desperately longed for, and are you now addicted to the pleasure?

This is why growing and maintaining a relationship with God is so important. For a husband and wife, though it may be hard, they may be able to work through the roughest of times and bring themselves together again intimately. However, for an unmarried individual, it is not so easy. For those of you who are single, although we have already stated that you should not bond yourself sexually with anyone until you are married, don't count yourself out of the number, but rather, count yourself as one who God wants to intimately take care of himself. Trust me, he understands the need within you and the desire for human touch; he made you. But until the day you become wed to someone, your most intimate parts should belong to you and God alone because he's the only one who will be able to keep you satisfied if you let him. However, before jumping the broom, you should seek to find yourself complete in God, or you will find yourself searching for satisfaction everywhere other than at home.

You obviously don't have to ask me how I know.

For those who still don't believe in the whole "no sex before marriage" rule or saving yourself for just one person, you might argue, since my husband and I had already made the conscious decision to separate from each other, what was wrong with "exploring my options"? I agree that, in my mind, I was no longer a part of this marriage, which, for a while, I used as justification for why I felt no guilt; I wasn't even wearing my wedding ring at the time. However, we were not yet divorced, and I wasn't married to the guy that I was indulging in sexual pleasure with. So though you may argue against abstaining from pre-marital sex, there is no argument against adultery. No matter how you slice it, no matter how justified I felt about it, it was wrong, and I was guilty.

Here's what the Bible says about it:

HEBREWS 13:4 (MSG)

4 Honor marriage, and guard the sacredness of sexual intimacy between wife and husband. God draws a firm line against casual and illicit sex.

God honors marriage and esteems it as high as Christ loving the church. "The two shall become one flesh" is what the scripture says. So when you step outside of your marriage and engage in sexual activity with someone else, you have spiritually divided yourself and have become spiritually wed to another person. In some countries, having sex with someone means you have now been given to that person. Even here in America, a judge will ask, before granting a divorce, if you have consummated the marriage. Sex is a serious, intimate act that shouldn't be taken lightly or had casually. Ask God to show you other things to satisfy you before turning to sex because, even if you don't think so, it will dramatically and permanently alter your life.

The days went on, and I became more and more attached to him, not realizing how deep it was until the day he left to go home, and I cried the entire night. His leaving meant that I was now going to be forced to step back into the reality of my unsatisfied life. With nothing and no one to take my mind off reality and still no desire to fix my marriage, I was, once again, forced to deal with my personal demons. The next couple of weeks opened my eyes to just how broken I really was and the pain became so unbearable, I decided that I needed some time off and away from everything and everyone. The truth was, I needed time away with God. There was no mistaking the fact that I had allowed my life to spiral out of control and confusion had taken over my mind, while pain had taken over my heart. Music was against it from the beginning. He did not understand why I had to go alone and questioned how long I would be gone and where I would be going. Simply put, I let him know that, if he ever wanted me to even think about making things work between us, he would just have to be okay with it. I was going to go no matter what he said. The plans I made were to be alone with God, but the deep desire to see Skillz again had been invading my thoughts, so I traded my original plans for the opportunity to be alone with him, at least, for a little while. Knowing that what I was doing was a sin, I was so desperate for happiness, and I had become so consumed with him that I was ready to alter my entire world just to be where he was. What I had allowed my heart to feel for him, though it was completely wrong, was completely real. However, because it was all formulated out of sin and deception, it was also killing me from the inside out.

This all escaped my mind once I saw his face and my heart began to beat harder than the rhythmic pounding of a bass drum in the middle of a parade. Sinfully in love was what I called it. I justified it, however, by convincing myself that, though this was wrong, it was okay because Music and I didn't want to be together anyway. I hadn't even been wearing my ring. After getting settled into what would be home for the next couple of days, I proceeded with allowing the first half of my time away with God to officially turn into time away with him. Here I was again, indulging in being uninhibited, getting high, and having sex, far away from home ... and I loved every minute of it. Only this time, though, God had had enough.

When I opened my eyes the next morning, I looked around the sun-filled hotel room that had been littered with tossed clothes in a moment of intoxicated lust, and I felt ... lost. The night before was a blur, though I remembered enough to know what I had done again. I could not, however, explain my feelings. As I looked over and saw him ironing his shirt and watching television, this overwhelming sense of loneliness came over me, followed by complete disgust. Feeling guilty and shamefully exposed, I couldn't even look at him in the same way I had just the night before. I pulled the sheets from the bed to hide myself and quickly skipped into the bathroom as a feeling of heaviness sat on my chest. As I leaned over the sink, my breathing became labored; I felt as if I was drowning, and my entire body was shaking. Looking up into the mirror ... I was so confused; I had no idea who was staring back at me. My identity had been lost in a sea of masks, lies, pain, and filth that I had tried to pass off as my true self. Not even a hot shower to scrub away the shame of it all could change what I was feeling; I had finally hit rock.

From the moment I jumped up to run to the bathroom, Skillz constantly asked me if I was okay, saying that I looked different. Though I wish I could have, I couldn't explain what was happening to me. There was no way to explain something that I didn't understand myself. I needed to get away. I needed to run away. I simply told him that I needed time alone, so for a few hours, I went off to find the very thing that I had gone there for in the first place — the beach. A slight fear of him thinking that I was unstable came over me, but for the first time, I could actually admit that I was, so my feelings totally outweighed that.

The air, though cooler because of the time of year, was warm enough to enjoy being outside, and the clouds, though heavy, held back the pending rain long enough to take a walk out onto the sand. As I walked closer to the water and inhaled the sounds and smells of the ocean, it became easier to breathe, and finally, I spoke. Though I began by admitting to God that I knew I was wrong, I also told him that I felt no remorse. He would have to change my heart and take me back home to Music because I didn't want to do it, neither was I willing to do it. I was open. I was honest. I left it in His hands.

I wanna do right, but I wanna do wrong.

I wanna be right, but what I feel is wrong.

I can't do wrong if I'm gonna be right,

So, God, help me do right

Because what I wanna do is wrong.

After standing in silence, looking out onto the endless waves for about ten minutes, it began to lightly rain, and a sadness fell on me. I felt undone and incomplete. Was that it? Was that what I had come for, or had I messed everything up by giving God's time and my body to someone else, yet again? Walking back toward my car, I stopped at a bench just at the top of the stairs that led up from the sand to put my shoes back on, and the rain slowed to a stop. I looked up at the sky with tears filling my eyes and said, "Say something to me." What happened next, though I can describe it, you would not fully understand, unless you were there and unless you were me. After my simple request, God clearly responded with, "You know I love you, right?" As simple as that may sound, it broke me down, and I doubled over and poured my heart out on that bench, as God continued to pour his love on me with words of affirmation and mercy, as the brightness of the sun broke through the dark clouds, both on the beach and within me. This moment was so surreal. After everything I had allowed to happen, the first thing he told me was that he loved me. He didn't talk to me about what I had done. He didn't speak on my current state. He didn't even demand I go home to my family, or threaten me with doom. He told me exactly what that thirteen-year-old, insecure, fatherless girl wanted to hear all along: *"I love you."*

In an instant, my entire disposition was changed. It was time to go home, and I actually wanted to go. Still overwhelmed and blinded by tears, I drove back to check out of my hotel room (a day early) and let Skillz in on the decision that I had made to leave. Finally, I was able to speak to him about what I had been feeling all morning and told him a small portion of what happened on the beach, without going into detail. Admittedly, letting him go was one of the hardest things I'd ever had to do, but after we sat and talked for hours, he said he understood ... he said. It was truly a bittersweet moment as I felt as if my heart was breaking and being put back together all at the same time. Crying half of the way home, my tears seemed to transition from one thought to the next, from pain to promise, from hurt to healing. Finally, I arrived home, tired, a bit overwhelmed, and regretful, but happy. Music had not come in from work yet, so though I had spoken to him while I was driving, I hadn't told him that I had decided to return home sooner than expected. He walked into the room, switched on the light, and found me sitting on our bed, smiling. His eyes locked on me in disbelief, and he yelled for my mom, ran into her room, and collapsed to his knees in laughter and relief. Surprisingly, I was just as happy and relieved to see him.

While I was away, he admitted that there were moments his hurt told him to leave, but his heart said no. Instead, he took the time to pray that God would heal my heart and mend our relationship. He was the reason my heart was changed. He was the reason I felt the desire to come back home. As I finally gave in to God, my prayer linked with the prayers he was already speaking on my behalf. This man loved me unconditionally, but I was too blinded by my pain and emotions to see it. Over the next couple of days, I explained to him what happened to me on the beach, reassuring him that, though the decision to come back home was completely God-inspired, I was committed to staying where I was supposed to be. Completely awed by the story of my God-encounter, Music said that he wanted to make a trip to the beach and experience this same thing. The very next weekend, which happened to be his birthday, we did just that. Dropping everything for the sake of our marriage, we placed our daughter in the loving arms of my mother and drove eight hours in the middle of the night to encounter God individually. Only this time, we did it together.

CHAPTER 7
Déjà Vu

Three months. It had been three months since I had come back home, and though Music and I hadn't really argued in all that time, I still felt lost. I had been suppressing my feelings, but there were days when I couldn't fight, and I would cry out in pain and deep confusion. Why did I feel so incomplete? Was I still dealing with the guilt and grief over losing my father after all these years? My heart was still healing, yes, but was it really breaking me down like this? Honestly, there were a number of situations that could have driven me to this state; I had been suppressing my feelings for years. I had felt trapped while living in my mother's house because I was still trying to figure out life and all the roles I had to play in it. I was also trying to completely rid myself of the feelings that still remained for Skillz, which proved to be harder than I thought. I believed that, after my encounter with God on the beach and the second trip I took with Music, I would have been completely turned around and done with Skillz and my scattered emotions altogether. Not so. I found myself hiding the truth of my feelings more often and lying to Music and my friends, in order to save myself from the embarrassment of sounding like a hopeless, desperate girl, crying out for a man who didn't want her. My lies masked how much pain I was in; I was still fighting alone, and it seemed, the harder I fought, the harder it got and the more it hurt. The worse pain was feeling as if a piece of my heart and soul belonged to someone else while striving to stay focused and dedicated to my relationship with my husband.

Trying to stay away, not stray away
Can't keep my mind away
Image pressed, implanted like a chip
Visions of the past making me trip
Extended vacation
Feelings of anxiety from separation
Deprivation is best
For the mind must rest
Can't test ... the water's too deep
No shallow end; one step, you sink

What made matters worse was, Music ended up asking me what happened between Skillz and me and how I was feeling about everything. My body felt as if it was going to implode or fold into itself, as if it had been hit by a boulder. Why would he want to know the details of something so painful? His response: He wanted to know exactly what he was up against, so he could know exactly how to fight. How could I say no to that? As uncomfortable as it was, I told him everything he wanted to know but spared him a lot of the dirty details. Confessing my sins to him out loud felt as if I was digging a grave for my reputation, my character, and his outlook on who he thought me to be before all of this had taken place. Surely, there would be no way that he would ever look at me the same or even respect and trust me anymore, after hearing the way his wife had been behaving, with no remorse. After my confession, I slipped back into a state of depression; my now wounded spirit was feeling worthless and unworthy to be loved by Music, God, or anyone else, for that matter. I lived with deep feelings of regret for allowing myself to mistreat Music and our daughter the way I had, and for all that I had done. Yet ... there were still times I wanted to call Skillz and fall into his arms just one last time. Some nights, I cried non-stop, begging God to have mercy on me and help me, but I felt as if nothing was happening. What I didn't realize at the time was that I wasn't losing. Yes, there were times I wanted to call him. Yes, there were times I wished he would say something to me. Yes, he was constantly on my mind or popped in at some of the most inopportune times, but I was winning. Just a few months prior, whenever I thought about Skillz, I would contact him immediately, just for an emotional fix. Now, though, he still ran across my mind and I still wanted to connect with him (and at times, I actually gave in), but I remained conscious of the agreement made between myself and God, and I always bounced back. The biggest difference was made when I finally decided to seek help, instead of fighting this demon alone. I wanted out. I wanted to be free, so my first step was admittance. Without revealing too much detail to a couple of my friends, I let them into the parts of me I had kept tucked away, and much to my surprise, they stood by me, prayed for me and talked me off the ledge during those times I felt I was going to jump.

The tie that Skillz had on me was a hard knot to loosen, but slowly it became easier to stay away, and I was contacting him less and less. Aside from my personal efforts, there was also a coldness that developed between us, and it separated us further. He didn't talk to me the same way he used to. He didn't respond to me the same way he used to. There was this "I don't care" attitude he displayed whenever I spoke to him about what concerned me, and I didn't understand it. It hurt, but maybe God had allowed it, knowing that, if he would have expressed any interest in me, it would have been next to impossible to keep my promise and free myself of the ties that bound me to him.

Author's Love Note: *Can I be real with you? That part about God maybe allowing this to happen so that I could get free ... came to mind as I was writing. Never count yourself out! I know it may not seem that way right now, but if you are fighting, if you are trying, if you are resisting, you are winning! It often takes some time to receive complete deliverance from the things that bind us, especially if they're connected to another person. Don't look at your situation for what it is and say you will never beat it because you keep falling. If you fall nine times, get up ten! Keep getting up! The thing you must remember is that you will come out on the other side, if you stay focused on God. I don't care if you have to cry out to God every night — STAY THERE! He promised time and time again that he would be with you in the darkest of times. He even urges us in His word to not worry about the things that concern us; let him handle it instead.*

My all-time favorite scripture says it like this:

Isaiah 43:1-2 (NLT)

1 But now, O Jacob, listen to the Lord who created you.

O Israel, the one who formed you says,

"Do not be afraid, for I have ransomed you.

I have called you by name; you are mine.

2 When you go through deep waters,

I will be with you.

When you go through rivers of difficulty,

you will not drown.

When you walk through the fire of oppression,

you will not be burned up;

the flames will not consume you.

Here's even more reassurance:

John 16:33 (MSG)

33 "I've told you all this so that trusting me, you will be unshakable and assured, deeply at peace. In this godless world, you will continue to experience difficulties. But take heart! I've conquered the world."

1 Peter 5:7 (AMP)

7 Casting all your cares [all your anxieties, all your worries, and all your concerns, once and for all] on

Him, for He cares about you [with deepest affection, and watches over you very carefully].

With promises such as these to look forward to, how could I not take God up on his offer? Don't believe the enemy when he whispers to you that this is how it will always be! These (and other) verses clearly state that trusting and depending on God will get you out of the hardest places in your life! It will be difficult, it will hurt, it will be hard, but it will be worth it!

To all of you who have overcome, passed through the water and the fire, found that light at the end of the tunnel, and have been delivered from one, a few, or all of those things that bound you ... doesn't it feel good to be FREE? Now go encourage and help somebody else!

With Music and I finally on the same side again, we were now able to make better decisions for ourselves and our future. We decided to spend the next few months building ourselves emotionally, spiritually, financially, and physically, then prepared to move out on our own once again. Everything was going as planned until I became very ill in May and a trip to the doctor revealed that the way I had been feeling was not because of a stomach bug or food poisoning. Dr. Katie came back into the exam room and asked me if a positive pregnancy test would be a good thing or a bad thing — a question I really didn't know how to answer at the time. What did she mean *pregnant?* This was not what I had gone in for. I wasn't even able to get pregnant! For the past eight years, since my daughter had been born, I had not been able to conceive another child. Although Music and I had not been "trying," there was nothing we were doing to prevent it either. I lived with pain daily; sometimes it was so severe I had to be rushed to the emergency room with no real understanding as to what the cause was. After countless trips to doctors' offices and emergency rooms, they were all able to identify the problem: My reproductive organs were the cause of both my pain and my infertility. Great. So not only was I unstable, unhappy, and useless, but I also couldn't provide my husband with the family he wanted or my baby girl with the "company" she always cried for. Over the years, this was the basis of so many arguments, as I was so deeply hurt and Music didn't know how to comfort me. The psychological torment I went through was fueled by feeling like the very thing that made me a woman was taken away from me and replaced with physical pain. Surely, this was my punishment for abusing and giving away my body the way that I had for so long.

I was convinced that there had to be a mistake, but the blood test results that would come just a couple days later would prove that, not only was I pregnant, but I was about eight weeks along. How was this possible? Every doctor had told me that my condition would pretty much make it impossible to conceive any more children naturally. Not only that, I had been religiously taking the birth control pills my doctor had given me to regulate my system. No matter how hard I tried to fight the reality of what was happening, it was true.

I was alone on that trip to the doctor, so there was no one there to calm my fears. No one was there to give me reassurance, and no one else was there who was in on the secret. All the way home, I cried. For years, I had begged and pleaded with God to allow me to conceive another child, but when I said I didn't want it, it finally happened. *"Don't you know I can't handle this right now? I'm not ready for this! Why are you doing this to me? Why are you doing this to another child?"* Afraid of Music's reaction, I danced around the news when he asked me about my appointment once he came home from work. Eventually, he figured out what I was trying not to say. "You're pregnant?"

Much to my surprise, he was happy. Little by little, we revealed the news to our family and friends, who were all just as happy and excited as Music, while I remained in shock. Here I was, back in my mother's house, in the very same room where I had been shamefully impregnated with my first daughter, my projected due date was a day before her birthday, and I would soon find out that I was having another girl. I felt like I had stepped into the Twilight Zone. This was serious déjà vu, and I was terrified.

Sitting and thinking; quiet, no speaking.

Meditating? Not quite.

Just thinking about life.

Visions of the past flash like Polaroids

Still shots of forget-me-nots ...

Every thought and fear that broken seventeen-year-old girl experienced came back full-force. Depression gripped me again, to the point where I had a hard time being happy about my pregnancy, which drove Music to anger. He didn't understand the depth of my pain. The way he saw it was, though we may not have been in the place we wanted to be, we were together, we were married, and this was something only God could have allowed. I just couldn't see it. There were nights I could not sleep, due to anxiety. There were nights where my mother had to come into our room and calm me down because I had been crying for hours and could not pull myself together. There were nights (and days) where I just couldn't move or speak. During these moments, I felt I was even less of a mother to my daughter than I had ever been. She would want to talk and play, but I just couldn't give her the attention she needed, and it made my heart hurt. To make matters worse, the doctors became concerned for both my health and the health of my unborn baby girl because my body was responding negatively to my stress. I was too far gone in my emotions to manage it, and so, not only did I have to quit my job sooner than expected, but ultimately, the doctors made the decision to deliver her in December, three weeks early and three days before my birthday — what had I done? I was given steroid shots to help the development of her lungs, but what if she wasn't okay, all because of me? The thought terrorized my mind until three o'clock in the afternoon on December 27th, when I finally saw her. She was pink, tiny, and had the most beautiful eyes, but most of all, she was healthy.

I will never forget that day or the day I finally brought her home. It was my birthday, which had fallen on a Sunday that year. That afternoon, I was lying in our bed, when my daughter walked into the room. She had just returned home from church with my mom. She had this huge smile on her face because she had missed me and was excited to see the baby. As she sat down in the rocking chair, she asked to hold her little sister, and of course, I said yes. Tears of joy filled my eyes and a love I never thought I would feel for both of my girls filled my heart as I watched them gently rock in the chair as the light from the window filled the room. From the moment I placed the baby in her arms, this smile came across her face, as if every hurt had been erased, and every question had been answered in that one moment. Little did she know that, in that one moment, God had answered a million prayers for me as well.

CHAPTER 8
Chapter One

Genesis 1:1-4 (KJV)

1 In the beginning God created the heaven and the earth.

2 And the earth was without form, and void; and darkness was upon the face of the deep. And the Spirit of God moved upon the face of the waters.

3 And God said, Let there be light: and there was light.

4 And God saw the light, that it was good: and God divided the light from the darkness.

At the beginning of this book, I presented to you a girl, a girl who was without form and void. A girl who would soon be overcome with darkness that covered the depths of her heart and soul. A girl who didn't know who she was, where she belonged, or where to go. No, she may not have been abandoned or unloved, but she was lost and did not have an identity. At the beginning of this book, this girl was the unformed earth. Toward the middle of this book, I talked to you about the different accounts of hardship, pain, moments of confusion, and difficulties this girl faced, all from the ties that had her bound. Though each account gave way to what seemed like an elevation of darkness, one thing remained constant: God stayed with this girl, wherever she went. He remained on the inside of her, ready to take action and pull her out of darkness whenever she would call on Him. In the middle of this book, this girl was the water that God's spirit moved over.

Now, here we are at the end of this book, and you have been made aware that this was a true, unadulterated story and that this girl was me. Walking through the chapters of my life, you have read about some of my darkest times, and one of the most painful soul ties imaginable. However, what you were also given insight to was what happened the day the light broke through and came forth. Then one day, as I stood on the beach, God poured his love into me (reassuring me that I had not gone so far that his love could not lift me from the dark waters where I had been sinking deep). He spoke the words "Let there be." From that day, I have fought and fought to be freed from the ties by never again leaving God's presence, by never again allowing myself to be dragged out to sea without knowing how to swim or without a life preserver. Since that day, God has been able to see the light that shines from within me, and since that day, He has called me good. Good enough to continue to bless me in the areas I once took for granted. Good enough to allow me the opportunity to fix many of the situations that felt impossible to fix (my mind included) and grow from every lesson he was teaching me in the midst of it all. He even called me good enough to allow me to use the words that He speaks through me to encourage, not just myself, but others as well.

The purpose of this book was not simply to tell a story. The purpose of this book was not just to get some things off my chest or to let you in on the secrets of who I really was or the behind-the-scenes actions. My purpose for writing this book was to help those who have or are having a hard time identifying themselves, so they have tried to find their identity in things and people. For years (even in the years following the last part of this story), I tried to find my identity in my style and fashion, in being a mom, a wife, a vixen, a friend, a business woman, a singer, a writer, a fitness instructor, even a minister-in-training. It wasn't until January 2, 2017 that I was finally able to hear God clearly as to why I could never find myself in any one of those things. These things were simply titles or labels, but they were not identities. For far too long, I had allowed people to make me feel unstable because I could never stay interested in just one thing. I wanted to do everything. Although some thought it was pretty cool that I could learn how to do things pretty easily, others made me feel as if I were scatter-brained and unfocused. This made enjoying life, my talents, and discovering my interests difficult because I based life-decisions on the words and opinions of others who simply didn't understand me. I allowed my low self-esteem, guilt, and depression to define me, and that became my reasoning for why I did many of the things I did. But this was not who I was; this was simply the person I had become.

I was never supposed to choose one thing to identify myself. I was always supposed to see who God made me to be and be that person in the midst of all of these things. Finally, after years of searching for myself, I got it. It didn't happen right away. I would pray for strength for days on end sometimes, but those were the times God was trying to remind me that I actually had all of the strength and power I needed, already within. All I had to do was remember who I was to Him and who He was in me.

Author's Love Note: *More often than not, it is the strongest people that feel the weakest in moments of pain and discomfort. Everyone would tell me how strong I was, and there were times when I believed it, but then, there were other times when I wondered if they realized who they were talking to. In those times, I asked God to give me strength, and these are some of the scriptures that he reminded me of. I repeated them to myself over and over again until I believed it and was strong enough to get up.*

Even now, I keep them as reminders:

Isaiah 40:28-31 (KJV)

28 Hast thou not known? hast thou not heard, that the everlasting God, the Lord, the Creator of the ends of the earth, fainteth not, neither is weary? there is no searching of his understanding.

29 He giveth power to the faint; and to them that have no might he increaseth strength.

30 Even the youths shall faint and be weary, and the young men shall utterly fall:

31 But they that wait upon the Lord shall renew their strength; they shall mount up with wings as eagles; they shall run, and not be weary; and they shall walk, and not faint.

Psalm 27:1 (KJV)

The Lord is my light and my salvation; whom shall I fear? the Lord is the strength of my life; of whom shall I be afraid?

II Corinthians 12:8-10 (NLT)

8 Three different times I begged the Lord to take it away.

9 Each time he said, "My grace is all you need. My power works best in weakness." So now I am glad to boast about my weaknesses, so that the power of Christ can work through me.

10 That's why I take pleasure in my weaknesses, and in the insults, hardships, persecutions, and troubles that I suffer for Christ. For when I am weak, then I am strong.

Philippians 4:13 (KJV)

13 I can do all things through Christ which strengtheneth me.

These scriptures speak strength back into me whenever I need it. In your hardest and roughest times, search for scriptures that have the exact words that God would speak to your heart, in your situation. Search different versions of the Bible, search through different commentaries, search through books that others have written on what you're facing. The more you deposit goodness into you, the more you will be able to identify who you really are.

It was a brand new year, and I finally felt like myself. But if I had been searching for myself all these years, how did I truly know who I was? How I know is because I felt free. Music and I had been hit with situations that should have broken us faster than anything we had faced in years past, but we muscled through it all. One thing we were faced with, yet again, was the news that we were expecting our third baby. It was September, and we were preparing to move from our apartment into our first home, but the same two lines that had shown up thirteen years ago, in the bathroom stall at school, added a bit of extra excitement to the change that was getting ready to take place. This time around, however, I was filled with laughter and excitement. Music and I had been at odds for a couple of days, but once I let him in on the secret that left me full of laughter, he smiled from ear to ear as he embraced his wife who was, once again, carrying new life made from love. This time felt different because this time *was* different. My outlook was different, my faith was different, my attitude was different, and my self-esteem was different. The next month, however, all of that would be tested in the greatest way. Different obstacles came against us with the purchase of our new home, but we stood firm; we stood on God. Even with the ever-changing emotions that come along with carrying a child, I was able to find a piece of peace in the midst of it all, and the day came when we finally closed the deal.

Going through that stint of time, I admit, was pretty rough. However, I was determined to stay focused on the fact that God was strengthening us and working things out on our behalf. I had become a master of my emotions; I had never experienced this before, and it felt amazing. With my head and my heart in a better place, God was now able to speak to me, and I was finally able to understand the very thing he wanted me to see all along. The things I had done and been through or allowed myself to get caught up in did not define me, neither did my everyday titles or responsibilities or my gifts and talents. I finally understood why I could never find complete satisfaction in just one thing; I wasn't designed for just one thing. He told me I was an undefined vessel, able to be used for many purposes. I prayed and asked God to use me however he saw fit. Whatever capacity he needed me to be used in, I wanted to be willing. When he spoke the words "undefined vessel" to me, I finally understood, and the years of being lost in my true identity melted away in an instant. Finally, I was free. There had been many times where I had claimed freedom, but this time was real, and I could identify myself as that: Free.

That's why they call me Bird.

My prayer is that somewhere, within these pages, you read something that gave you a sense of hope that you are not alone in this journey that you are on. Know that it doesn't have to end in tragedy. Though it may feel isolating and lonely at times, God really is with you, for you, and on your side. Make a declaration with me: Whenever you feel (even a bit of) freedom, claim it. Say that this is what you are until it truly becomes the definition of who you are. Walk in freedom by learning to love who you are, learning to trust God to be all that he said he would be to you, and by asking him to allow the right people to walk into your life to replace the toxic ones. What I didn't realize until many years had gone by was that I couldn't fight alone. Keeping my fears, worries, frustrations, and concerns to myself drove me deeper and deeper into an unrealized isolation that caused me to feel abandoned and unable to be reached. I urge you to find someone you can confide in, who will pray with you and for you, who can help guide you through, and be the bridge you need to keep from falling into any more troubled waters. Not everyone in your life will be that bridge. Not everyone in your life will be the help or the support you need and want at times, and that is okay. Through the process of God remaking me, there have been some friends and family that I realize will not be able to take this part of my journey through life with me. Is it a comfortable transition? Not always. Is it making me stronger? Absolutely. In those places that I would have normally filled with the physical touch of a man or words of affirmation and reassurance from friends, I am learning how to depend on God alone to be the satisfaction I have been searching for all my life.

You who have read this book, who have overcome many of these adversities or more, I pray that you continue to walk in the truth and the strength that you have found. I pray that you never forget the dark place from where you came, so you will never again return, except to grasp the hands of those who feel as if they are sinking. Be a light to someone who is still trapped in darkness. Be the roadblock and the detour that keeps them from getting to that place of no return. Remember what it was like to be lost in the maze of your sin, fear, emotions, and pain, and show them the way out. You who have read this book, who is still searching for your true identity, while feeling like you are trapped by life, let me reassure you that there is a way out. There is a real peace that you can experience. There is a way to be free from the knots that feel as if they are choking the life out of you, like a noose. When you learn to love yourself beyond what you see, forgive yourself for what was and realize your identity is more than just what you do and your abilities. You will find that you, too, may be an undefined vessel, and that is a beautiful thing.

Ask me how I know.

Psalm 18:20-24 (MSG)

20 God made my life complete

when I placed all the pieces before him.

When I got my act together,

he gave me a fresh start.

21 Now I'm alert to God's ways;

I don't take God for granted.

22 Every day I review the ways he works;

I try not to miss a trick.

23 I feel put back together,

and I'm watching my step.

24 God rewrote the text of my life

when I opened the book of my heart to his eyes.

Throughout this book, I shared pieces of poetry I have written over the years that stretch across each story. This final poem came to me right in the midst of the pain I was dealing with, but it speaks of something that I wanted or was anticipating because I was not yet experiencing it. I believe God was trying to speak life into me, through my own words. Just as God used my poetry to speak to me and be a catalyst in guiding me to my freedom, I pray you, too, find the very thing that will walk you into yours.

She Is … I Am …

She is death, bondage, and disease.

She is not me, and I am not she.

She is a loose cannon; one wrong move and boom.

Words spit fire, and the pain runs deep,

Leaving innocent bystanders to bleed internally.

Who you were and what you did didn't matter in her mind.

She even burned her own mother two or three times.

Once … twice … three times a lady?

All the characteristics of a female,

But as true as that may be, a lady she was not.

She was hot; she let too many hands dig in that pot

Wanna show 'em all what she's got,

What she was capable of and how tasty she really was,

So one, after another ...

Them, him, and his brother?

Though many times she wouldn't go all the way,

Pieces of her would stay where she laid

With men of all ages, faces, and grade,

But that wasn't enough,

Much deeper was her lust

Than to just lay down with them

And get up in disgust.

It was a must

To find something more that she could trust,

To give her that rush that she longed for so much.

So a new set of friends she searched for and found.

One was a toxin, one grew from the ground.

Both at the same time altered her mind,

And gave her that high she thought she'd never find

A little puff-puff-give and a sip of Hennessey

Turned into a bottle of Bacardi and a dime all for she,

But there was no conflict cuz she wasn't an addict.

At anytime she wanted, she could stop it.

She could give it up.

She could let go. She could drop it,

But she wouldn't cuz she really couldn't,

So she found herself caught up in it,

That life full of things she couldn't mention, but she did it.

Her life, spiraling downward, and it just wouldn't stop

Going nowhere fast, until she finally hit rock

Bottom ... for her, this was it.

No reason left to live.

No reason to try, just die.

No reason left to exist.

Many times, she decided to take her life,

Even when she found there was another one inside ... of her.

In her womb, another life grew,

Terrifying the thought of she times two.

She thought, Get rid of number two.

No use burdening the world with the two of you, right?

A secret it remained, but one day, things changed.

The doctor can't keep her secret cuz, at seventeen, she was underage.

Her plans for a life free of "mini-she" failed.

When she was told she would die on the table as well ... if she did it

Great ... two birds, one stone ... let's get it.

But God had other plans. With She, he wasn't finished.

She had a calling on her life. He wanted her to see,

Filled with pain, shame, and grief, but He had his hand on She.

Such a hard outer shell, but on the inside, screaming, "HELP ME!"

Once on her way to hell, but somebody prayed for She.

So who is "She"?

I am not She

She is not me

But ... She is who I used to be.

I am who she has become.

So you ask, what's the difference between me and She?

I told you, she is death, bondage, and disease.

And I ... am FREE.